WOODLAWN
Giants

ROBERT R. WILLIAMS

Copyright © 2024 Robert R. Williams.

All rights reserved. No part of this book may be reproduced, stored, or transmitted by any means—whether auditory, graphic, mechanical, or electronic—without written permission of both publisher and author, except in the case of brief excerpts used in critical articles and reviews. Unauthorized reproduction of any part of this work is illegal and is punishable by law.

ISBN: 979-8-89419-437-0 (sc)
ISBN: 979-8-89419-438-7 (hc)
ISBN: 979-8-89419-439-4 (e)

Because of the dynamic nature of the Internet, any web addresses or links contained in this book may have changed since publication and may no longer be valid. The views expressed in this work are solely those of the author and do not necessarily reflect the views of the publisher, and the publisher hereby disclaims any responsibility for them.

One Galleria Blvd., Suite 1900, Metairie, LA 70001
(504) 702-6708

CONTENTS

Acknowledgements v

Chapter 1   The Pines, Bobby Knievel, And West Memphis 1

Chapter 2   Church Visitors, Food, And Dirty Windows 15

Chapter 3   Big Phil and the Gang, Our Sports Complex,
Deer Fishing, Florida Ball, and the Redbirds 30

Chapter 4   Parents Make Mistakes Too 45

Chapter 5   Nasa Comes To Town, Basketballs, Pie,
And A Tornado 51

Chapter 6   Bayous, Bar Pits, And Cutoffs 57

Chapter 7   Injuries in the Neighborhood 68

Chapter 8   Jobs 79

Chapter 9   Music, My First Concert, Lynyrd Skynyrd,
Riverside Speedway, And a Snipe Hunt 84

Chapter 10 Restaging Accidents, Those Pesky Pears,
And an Apple 92

Chapter 11 Operation "Now and Later" 100

Chapter 12 Television, Simple Pastimes 109

Chapter 13 All Things Must Pass and the Circle of Life 113

About the Author 121

ACKNOWLEDGEMENTS

I would like to thank Jessa Amores and The Ewing Publishing for their assistance in publishing this second edition of Woodlawn Giants.

Dawn Heath Thomas, for supporting me in proofreading the manuscript.

Deborah Perdue and Tara Thelen from Illumination Graphics for the cover design.

Mothers and fathers on Woodlawn, Janice and Gina, and the boys the Woodlawn Giants.

Me and Momma at Christmas 1973.

Chapter 1

THE PINES, BOBBY KNIEVEL, AND WEST MEMPHIS

The Pines, 1968

Daddy and Mr. Rick planted some pines. They are still there to this day, standing tall, looking good and high in the sky. But when they planted them, they were basically just small seedlings about a foot tall. I can remember them straight in a line, like little green soldiers standing in formation. I also recall one winter when there was a huge winter storm, and the little soldiers were completely covered in snow, and I thought to myself there's no way they can survive this. The poor little trees are doomed. The little young green soldiers will surely freeze to death or suffocate under this avalanche of unseasonal white powder. But the snow melted, spring came, and the little trees survived. These would grow into what I now call the Woodlawn Giants. Each tree to me symbolizes the giants and grown men that we the boys who grew up on Woodlawn became. Brothers Big Phil and Rod Spicer, and their cousin Perry White, the three Williams brothers, me Brad and Bruce, the other Spicer Clan brothers Mark and Ricky, Steve and Doug Sutton, Tony and David Busby, Doug White, Keith Dial, and a host of others. I look back on that time with fond memories. The friendships we built have stood the test of time. Every time I go home, I look forward to reconnecting with the gang. Unfortunately, as time goes on, we see each other less and less as life gets in the way. And although we have experienced some of our friends passing, the memories live on, and the trees are still standing.

The Ten-Mile Bayou, a boy on his bike, and a jump

"He's gonna do it," T-bone pronounced to his little bro, Doug. "Man, after the go-cart crash, you would have thought he learnt his lesson. I always said he was an accident looking for a place to happen, but it seems like now he is always looking for a place to make an accident."

Batman and his tricked-out bike 1966.

Many of the neighborhood kids had gathered where the Ten-Mile West Memphis Bayou met Woodlawn Street in the eastern part of West Memphis, Arkansas, located on a flood plain of the Mississippi River directly west of Memphis, Tennessee. After a week of practice jumping on ramps built with stacks of bricks and flat boards, the jumpers had decided to raise the stakes and elevate their game, to do something more audacious. Years before Evel Knievel failed to jump Snake River

Canyon, the Woodlawn boys had chosen their own attempt to jump a body of water, the Ten-Mile Bayou.

Bicycles were a big thing back then. Every kid had one, and there were all types of methods of tricking them out. The first time I really decorated a bike was for a special occasion. Momma made sure I was decked out for the kindergarten contest where she dressed me up as Batman. For my bike, a Schwinn, she attached balloons to the handlebars, and colored paper mâché around the spokes of the tires. As we got older, we modified and decorated our own bikes. For sound effects, we would take playing cards and attach them to the spokes for that flapping noise when we started pedaling. The structural modifications the boys made to their bikes were influenced by the Harley choppers popular of that time. We would take the forks off one bike, remove our front tire, attach those removed forks to the original forks, thus extending them in length, and reattach the tire. We then added a tall sissy bar, a banana seat, some tassels for decorations, and you were in business. However, these fancy prototypes might look snazzy, but they were not built for jumping. That lesson was learned the hard way as a crash and burn reminiscent of Evel Knievel's landing at Caesar's Palace repeated itself right in front of 621 East Woodlawn. This was when T-bone's little brother Doug decided to jump his tricked-out bike, and it didn't end well. The impact from the landing snapped the extended fork, off came the wheel, the bike nosedived, and, over the handlebars, Doug went down in a tumble.

"Doug, Doug, you, okay?" cried Bruce.

Getting up and shaking it off. "I'm hurt a little bit but mostly hungry," mumbled Doug.

It was then a hard lesson learned that these tricked-out chopper bikes were good for riding around and looking sharp but not so good for jumps. The boys collectively decided that more solid and dependable models for jumping with lower center of gravities were better for trick riding and jumping. In other words, leaving their bikes in store-bought configuration and not modified for show. Speaking of injuries and accidents, Doug was second only to yours truly, me in that dubious category. More on that later.

Ten-Mile Bayou site of the famous unsuccessful jump attempt by Bobby Knievel and where countless other escapades took place.

The boys, being democratic and fair, implemented a competition to determine who would be the one who had the honor of making the jump over the bayou. They had a jumping contest on who could jump the farthest. That individual would win the honor of jumping the bayou. The competition ended in a tie between me, known as Cobb, and my cousin visiting from Memphis, Keith. How to decide the winner? No rock paper scissors for something this important, but instead out came the baseball bat. When playing a sandlot pickup game of baseball, the way of determining who got to bat first was a ritual involving a baseball bat. One player from one team tossed the bat to another on the opposing team. Wherever the bat was caught was the starting point. The opposing players would then, with alternating grabs on the bat, either a full grip or scissor, work their way up the handle of the bat and the one who ended up covering the base of the bat would win. I was the winner (if being the one to jump the bayou could really be described as a winner), and the rest of the jumpers became the pit and construction crew as well as responsible for putting the word out throughout the hood to generate an audience for the event.

Jump day came, and the construction crew built the ramp that I would use to jump the bayou. The terrain of the bayou was a steep incline that would give the jumper the required speed to level out very briefly before hitting the ramp and making his jump across the body of water. That murky water was more reminiscent of a moat complete with swamp creatures such as water moccasins and snapping turtles. These prehistoric-looking turtles were more like small alligators with shells, and if they bit you, as legend went, they would not let go until the sound of thunder, and that could be a long time. Also, nothing clear about this water—it was nasty, murky, and dark. Everything seemed to be in order as a crowd of curious kids had gathered on the jump side of the bayou to watch the jump. The game and ante had been raised. It was one thing to watch the so-called bigger kids jump on ramps onto the streets, but this was something new and even more exciting.

"That boy is crazy, ain't no way he is gonna make it to the other side," declared Janice nicknamed Skillet.

"Yes, he will. I have seen him jump dem ramps out front and he can fly like an eagle," added Doug.

"I bet he don't make it and crashes jus' like Evel Knievel always done," Janice retorted.

"I bet you ten marbles he does make it, good ones," Doug boasted.

"She don't play with marbles, she's a girl. All she gots is cooties," teased Bruce.

"She ain't no girl like normal girls. Bobby calls her Skillet, says she tuff like a boy and mean as a snake," added Bill.

"I do got some marbles because I keep winnin more and more off these dumb bets you boys keep making. Speakin of marbles, all you so-called smart boys, seems like you lost your marbles," boasted Skillet.

"What you are talking about, Skillet, I ain't lost no marbles. I have em right here in my pocket next to my cinnamon roll," declared Doug.

"I think she is speaking figures instead of literals. Momma taught me those fancy smancy words," Bruce pontificated.

"What is dat, Bruce?" Bill inquired.

"You clowns hush up. What Bru is saying is Skillet is speaking figuratively about all your respective insanity levels, not literally about real marbles. Must think she is a psychologist or sumthing. We can call her Doctor Skillet from now on. And, Doug, if you stole the last cinnamon roll, Hattie gonna have something for you when we go home," Steve reckoned.

"Better hope it ain't a hug and a kiss. Las time she asked Doug to do that, Doug said he couldn't, that he had a tummy ache," laughed Bill.

"Whatever, it's a bet Dr. Skillet. Ten marbles it is, and they better be good ones," declared Doug.

"It's a bet, and as for their condition, they better be good enuff, if I lose. They are the same ones I won off you last week when I bet you dat you couldn't go two ires without saying you were hungry. That was the easiest ten marbles I ever did win," teased Skillet.

Suddenly, a loud voice made an announcement. Using one of those long cardboard tubes used for mailing things as a makeshift microphone, Keith opened the event.

"Ladies and gentlemen, and Skillet (a slight to Janice). You are about to see one of the most spectacular events to happen right here on your street. My cousin Bobby is gonna jump dis ditch with dat there bicycle right before your very eyes. Fellas, lets git the show started," declared Keith.

At that time, my supporting cast, Doug and Bruce, one on each side holding the handlebar grip, proudly rolled out my bicycle and steered it right up to the edge of the bayou.

"Real funny, Keith. Now where is your crazy cuz? Dat bike ain't gonna jump itself," probed Skillet.

"And now, Bobby Knievel," Keith announced.

I then walked out from the back porch and made my grand entry for the event. I was, along with some of the other kids, known as somewhat of a daredevil, so I was a natural choice. My protection consisted of wearing football pants to protect my knees (kids always seemed to have skinned-up knees those days), a T-shirt, makeshift cape, and a football helmet. There had been no practice jumps, so everyone there would witness firsthand an original attempt to make a successful jump. I mounted my bicycle and positioned myself for the jump but not before a small speech for the excited crowd.

"As you know, I was hurt bad last year in the crash on the go-cart that myself, Steve, and Doug built, but that is another story for another day. I am not afraid, and this should be easy. Thanks for coming out, and I'm ready to make the jump. Skillet, what you grinning about? What's so funny? Fellas keep her away from the ramp, no tellin what she might do, could be tampered wit already. Doug and Bru, go make a last-minute check of the ramp. I would hate to go flying down this hill and there be nothing to propel me to the other side," I ordered the pit crew.

Doug and Bruce went down and gave a thumbs up that the ramp was good to go and that the jump could commence. But easy it was not. The crew had built a good ramp, but geometry, projection, and angles were obviously not their strong suit. The problem was that a ramp built for a higher takeoff did not necessarily equate to allowing he jumper to travel farther but conversely just go higher and travel a shorter distance. So, I backed up my bike, started furiously peddling toward the incline, and down the side I went toward the ramp. I leveled out briefly before hitting the ramp, and up but not across I went. My bike in a vertical position, I landed, back tire first, in the middle of the bayou and was thrown backward butt first into the water. My pit crew was there for me and, quickly aware of the dangers of the creatures in the water, bravely retrieved me and my bike from the water. Although a failed attempt and a bruised ego I shook it off, and it was on to the next adventure. Just another day on Woodlawn.

Lay of the land, from a bluff to a floodplain

Me and my brothers. Love Momma's white socks.

I was born in 1960 in Memphis, Tennessee, the Bluff City, and lived for a short time in South Memphis, on Latham Street, surrounded by churches. Shortly thereafter, we moved west across the mighty Mississippi River from Memphis, Tennessee, to West Memphis, Arkansas. West Memphis, Arkansas, not to be confused with Memphis, Tennessee, is in Northeast Arkansas, just across the Mississippi River, and us natives jokingly refer to it as Left Memphis because when you look at it on a map, it is left of Memphis. The thing you remember most about West Memphis is the number of trucks you see at the many truck stops as you drive by on I-40/55. It really is one big truck stop. It is also referred to as the Crossroads of America. St. Louis, Missouri, may be a gateway, but West Memphis is another of those few cities in America where two major interstates, one running east and west, I-40, and the other running north and south, I-55, intersect. The other big attraction is of course the dog track. Why people would bet money on which greyhound, out of a pack of greyhounds, would win a race chasing an electric rabbit named Rusty beyond me. But apparently, it was an attraction and still stands to this day.

We had no fences, once was wide open, what a backyard it was!

My family set up shop on 621 East Woodlawn, and what an awesome place it was, at least to us. Our street had two entry points and is best described as a large U-shape horseshoe with a west side and an east side both connecting to Hamilton. The amazing thing about our property was our backyards were extended. The property lines blended into the huge church lots working their way from East Barton back toward Woodlawn, thus providing us boys with a huge area for the sport of the season, mostly football and baseball. Looking out from our back porch, one could see wide open space to the immediate front bordered by the bayou on the right side extending all the way to East Barton. That view is blocked now by the huge pine trees that run across the property line to the rear of the backyards. What were tiny two-feet saplings are now massive pines. Also, there have been fences constructed as well. No longer is the massive playground afforded to current residents like it was for us, early first-time buyers and settlers. Over time, fences, rules, and people change, and new barriers just get in the way. The houses backed up to the property now seem completely separated from what was for us a huge open space. What a waste of real estate. Why is that lot still undeveloped? There should be a park there for the residents. We played there; the kids who live there now should be able to play there.

People were/are different, and that's okay

Our town was segregated. There were two sides of town divided by Broadway, where the south side was mostly Black, and the north, divided into east and west regions, was mostly White. As for our street, most of the kids on Woodlawn were the same. They dressed the same, liked the same kind of things, and were White. I knew there were Black people living close by, but they may as well have been a thousand miles away. They stayed on their side of town, and we stayed on ours.

It was in school that I became more acquainted with Blacks, and like us, they were very similar in that they all dressed the same, basically talked the same, and were Black. This was the result of living in a very segregated society, defined by the color of one's skin. I can remember when walking home from school when I was attending East Junior High how every day I was reminded of this segregation. As we would be walking east, back toward Woodlawn, one of the first intersections we would come to would be Fourteenth Street and East Barton. Most White kids would head straight, a few that lived close by would go left and right, but every single Black kid would take that right and head south toward their side of town.

I really thought nothing much about it until one day when I was in the sixth grade at Maddux Elementary, a new kid showed up to school. I was playing box hockey with my best friend Jimmy Gately when the new kid at school approached us. And what a shock. He was Black but dressed entirely different than anyone else at school both Black and White. And when he talked, he sounded entirely different than anyone in that school, again Black or White. He said hello and that his name was Anthony, but everyone called him Tony. Tony told me he had just recently moved to West Memphis and was from San Diego, California.

We became fast friends. This experience opened my eyes a bit. This is how prejudices are effectively dealt with, real-life experiences where you figure out things yourself. Here was a kid unlike any kid in school I had ever met, but it didn't matter. He was a great kid, and we were good friends. He was just one example of how people could be different and cool at the same time. There were other examples of how people were different that were much closer to home and that would come from my own family, cousins to be exact.

People north of the Mason-Dixon line sho do talk funny

I had two sets of cousins, one from my father's side and the other from my mother's side, which also were living, breathing examples of differences in people. My cousins from up north in Michigan not only talked differently; they used different words. Who calls a soda pop? Who says *you guys* instead of *ya'll*. Who sings songs from *Sound of Music*? Who knows the words to "Que Sera, Sera"? Looking back, I am sure they were culture shocked just as much as we were. Their questions might be, "What in the world is the word *fixin*?" "Where is *down yonder*?" "How far is a *country mile*?" We may have sounded different when we talked and used different words, but we were family, and that trumped everything.

Williams and Hemmer kids

My other set of cousins from my father's side were the Hemmers. Uncle John was married to Dad's sister Aunt Doris. With Uncle John serving in the navy, his and Aunt Doris's kids were military brats. That meant at a young age, they had lived all over and would never be confused for kids as being from West Memphis, Arkansas. They stayed a few days, and before they left, all us kids were in a group photo. The picture of us in front of their car-pulled trailer depicts two different worlds. Look at the picture, and you be the judge of the contrast between these two groups of children. But that contrast is misleading and superficial. They might look different, but inside they were the same as us, just kids, and it did not take long for all of us to become thicker than thieves.

My fondest memory of that visit was when we were camping out in the backyard. We also had a trailer that fit on the back of Dad's truck but when not in use was perched on sawhorses. We had decided we would stay there for the night. Let's call it introducing our cousins to redneck camping. Pam and Brad, being the elders, divided the trailer down the center, where they were living all spacious and luxurious on one side, and myself, Bruce, Billy, and Kenny were crowded like sardines on the other. I swear I thought our little house for the night was gonna fall over. I wasn't too bright, but I did understand weight proportions from my time on a seesaw, so I demanded access to the other side. Firstly, because I wanted more room, and secondly, like I said, our side was lurching and about to fall over—at least I thought it was.

"I'm coming over there, it's too crowded on this side," I complained.

"No, you're not. You will stay right where you are," Pam directed.

Something in her demeanor convinced me she meant business, so I instantly capitulated.

"Yes, ma'am. Miss Pam understood!" I conceded.

To this day, we laugh about that, and I remind Miss Pam that I still understand.

Looking back on those times, what immediately comes to mind is just how different my children's lives were growing up than my own. To illustrate that difference, just from memory alone, here are the family names I remember on Woodlawn, and to this day I could show you their houses: the Freels, Musicks, Drennans, Lynches, Windhams, Johnsons, Whites, Marascos, Smiths, Busbys, Spicers (Mark and Ricky) Elmores, Procknaws, Vicks, Strange/Donaldsons, Williams, other Spicers (Phillip and Rodney), Suttons, Westons, Rogers, Wilburns, Roots, Clements and Lunsfords. That's twenty-four houses and family names I remember. Growing up in that world allows for lifelong friendships and acquaintances. Me and Ricky Spicer were in kindergarten together, and me and Chuck Davis were in the nursery at Ingram Boulevard Baptist Church together. I still have contact with some of them, but I remember all of them. Friends for life is a special thing.

Conversely, when looking at the life of my own children, it was different. Selena was born in West Memphis. We lived there a few years until I got stationed in California. She eventually ended up moving to Germany. As for Nathan, Alan, and Romi, all three were born in Tartu, Estonia, and the first thirteen, eleven, and nine years respectively of their lives, they lived in Europe. Another comparison that makes me laugh to myself is that once we were traveling through Germany and decided to visit a castle.

"You kids wanna go visit a castle?" I asked.

"Not another castle, I'm tired of seeing castles," Alan answered.

There weren't many castles in the vicinity of 621 East Woodlawn. The only ones I can remember were on television when there was a Walt Disney movie and, in the beginning, when Tinker Bell flies around with a castle in the background.

There are positive experiences for third culture children like my own children that I never experienced, but I would never trade that for my single culture upbringing in West Memphis. By third culture individuals, I am referring to people raised in a culture other than their parents or the culture of their country of nationality and live in a different environment during a significant part of their child development years. Nathan, Alan, and Romi were born in Estonia as American citizens and lived many years in Germany. Where is Estonia, you may ask? That question reminds me of a funny story that demonstrates how many who never leave the U.S. view things. My first time stationed in Estonia, I connected with an old friend from High School Pam Ball online and told her I was stationed in Estonia.

"Where are you stationed now?" asked Pam.

"I am in Estonia," I replied.

A few days later I heard from my friend.

"I looked all over a map in Tennessee, Arkansas, and Mississippi and couldn't find Estonia," declared Pam.

Well, I thought to myself, that is because it is a former part of the Soviet Union, a Baltic state next to the Baltic Sea bordering Russia and across the Gulf of Finland from Finland.

CHURCH VISITORS, FOOD, AND DIRTY WINDOWS

Church visitors

Our church was Ingram Boulevard Baptist Church. In 1946, it began as a mission of the First Baptist Church of West Memphis, Arkansas. The first parishioners met under a big oak tree, then in a tent, and in a few Sundays, they began meeting in a church member's home. On June 25, 1948, members of First Baptist Church met with the members of the mission, and Grace Baptist Church was organized. The property of Grace Baptist Church was eventually sold, and in July 1957, the name of Grace Baptist Church was changed to Ingram Boulevard Baptist Church. The new church building was completed in 1959. The new church in a brand spanking new building was waiting for us when we moved to West Memphis in 1960. Looking back, I wish it would have kept the name Grace. Ingram Boulevard sounds like something you might find on a monopoly board.

Well, we joined, and it was church on Sunday, church on Wednesday, and if a revival was in town, it was church on every day that ended in a Y. In other words, every single day. With that, it can be safely said we went to church a lot. And when summer came, we went to Vacation Bible School, and after that to Church Camp, and after that back to church. It was a cycle that seemed to never end. It wasn't always the preacher's teachings that provided the lessons of life, but things that happened as a result of people coming together, and everyday occurrences and activities associated with the church.

In the wink of an eye, you can leave this planet. I remember one time me and Keith were at a church camp and swimming at the pool. We were just kids, around six years old. Suddenly, one small boy started screaming that his brother was at the bottom of the pool. One of the camp counselors dove in and pulled this kid to the surface. The kid was unresponsive, and for all intents and purposes, he was dead, drowned. But God spared that child that day, and the counselor administering mouth-to-mouth resuscitation brought that kid back to life. Witnessing someone being revived was a significant emotional event for a six-year-old boy, and thank God that man saved that boy that day.

Another lesson learned was when our church was celebrating its tenth anniversary. There were tents outside set up with tables with all kinds of food for the feast to be held after our preacher Brother Henry Applegate's sermon. Right in the middle of the sermon, two young men, probably in their mid-twenties, as I remember them, walked into our church and crashed the sermon. You could have smelled them before you saw them, and they were not in their Sunday-go-to-meeting clothes, or maybe they were. Who decides what defines Sunday-go-to-meeting attire anyway? I never saw any men wearing three-piece suits, or women wearing dresses in the pictures in the Bible. Seems to me they were always wearing casual clothes like robes and sandals.

Maybe these fellas were more in tune with how to dress than we were. One of the guys had on a leather vest with no shirt underneath, wearing jeans and cowboy boots and a leather hat he was carrying by his side. *At least he took his hat off,* I thought to myself. The other guy also had jeans with holes in them, and a mesh shirt and, like the other one, was wearing cowboy boots, but instead of a cowboy hat, was wearing a Cubs hat. *Well,* I thought to myself, *if we deny him entry, it should be just because he's a Cubs fan.* Everyone knows God is a Cardinals fan, look at their titles. Yankee fans may disagree, but what does anyone north of the Mason-Dixon line know? Anyway, I digress. Back to our visitors.

The entry of these two men caused quite the stir in the congregation. Some folks didn't seem to care too much, while others were obviously not very accepting. These two gentlemen could have easily snuck quietly into the back and tried to keep a low profile. However, they took an opposite approach. If there was ever a more fitting description of *in front of God and country*, these two men fit the bill. In front of God and country, they marched right toward the front, found some free seats, and sat next to a group of old ladies. I think it is fair to say that these two older ladies were not happy with the new seating arrangement. Brother Applegate did not miss a beat and, with a slight nod of the head, acknowledged the two men. I was just curious as to why they had come inside from off the street since that was the first time that had ever happened since I had been going to church. Personally, I was always trying to find ways to get *out* of church, and these guys found a way to get *in*. *Why* was the immediate question? Suddenly, church got interesting for a change. This little social experiment was exciting to be a part of and observe.

Brother Applegate wrapped up the service and began the invitation where folks either gave their life to Christ or rededicated their lives. This ceremony would involve the preacher leaving his pulpit and walking down to the front of the congregation as the choir would quietly sing a hymn. The preacher, with arms open, would encourage members of the congregation to come forward. If unsaved, this was their opportunity to take that leap of faith and walk on down and give their life to God and decide to follow Jesus. If already saved and after some self-determination one thought they needed a new azimuth check, then he or she could come down and rededicate their life. In short, get back on the straight and narrow with the man upstairs. There was only one person that walked up front that day, and it was Brother Simon. *Wow*, I thought to myself, *if there was ever a person not in need of rededication, it would be that man*. He was a saint in my book, but more on him later.

Usually the invitation, and I will speak for myself, was of not much interest to me. What it really was most times was that light at the end of the tunnel. Thank God we are almost done and can get off this hard pew, which isn't good for sleeping, and go home to Momma's roast, carrots, and potatoes and then play outside. But this time it was different. I think the arrival of our guests from the outside world was some sort of divine bellwether and piqued the interest of everyone. I found myself more attentive, and instead of just hearing some music, I was listening to the song in the invitation and the actual words, "Softly and tenderly Jesus is calling… Come home, come home." I didn't walk down that day, but I believe I was impacted even more by what was happening around me. It made me question what I perceived as hypocrisy of certain members in the congregation. Additionally, it made me look critically at the church's practices and rituals. I wondered why the arrival of these two men and their intrusion into our congregation was one defined by mixed reactions. Should we not as a church have been more accommodating to our so-called fellow man? Later, after Momma helped me understand better what had just happened that day, I thought we, everyone including the preacher, could have done a much better job of welcoming these men into our church.

I started reflecting on the stories that Brother Gary had taught us in Sunday school. One was from the book of Matthew. One day, Jesus is walking along the beach of Lake Galilee and came across two men fishing on a boat, casting their nets into the lake. Jesus says to the two men, Simon and Andrew, "Come follow me, I will make you fishers of men." I am certain that Simon Peter and Andrew were not dressed up nicely that day and probably smelled like fish. Could our two guests not have been the next Simon Peter and Andrew? Could not the preacher have announced, "We have special guests today. Come inside, men, become part of our congregation and join us in serving the Lord"? Here was an opportunity to be inclusive and bring someone into the fold instead of shunning them, which is what some individuals, but not all, did that day. Church is not supposed to be some sort of club where only people dressed nicely can come on a routine basis, seeing the same old faces. I thought the doors were supposed to be open for all. The nets cast wide for all to come whether poor, wretched, or blind, or a host of other categories.

But back to that day. Brother Applegate announced the end of the service and invited the congregation, our two new guests included, to join him outside to celebrate the church's ten-year reunion. We all moved outside, and let me tell you, the amount of food outside made the regular potlucks we had on Wednesday night look like a snack. There were rows and rows of tables with every kind of food you could imagine. Then it dawned on me and became crystal clear. Our two new friends weren't in need of some preaching. They weren't starving for religion; they were starving for vittles and were simply hungry and in need of some food. But to use a fishing analogy, you need bait to catch fish. Perhaps the delicious food outside was the bait that lured these men into the sanctuary, and if just one iota of Brother Applegate's sermon resonated in those men and made them better persons, then I think everyone involved and God especially would be just fine with that.

Brother Applegate hushed the crowd and then asked Brother Simon to say a prayer and bless the food. Perhaps Brother Applegate bestowed that honor on Brother Simon since he was the only one who came forth in the invitation. Or perhaps it was prearranged, but either way, there could not have been a worse choice. And not because Brother Simon could not pray, but because he could pray exceptionally well albeit extremely long, and today he was the only thing standing between us and the food. Brother Simon was known by all of us boys as the one who said *dear God* in his prayers so many times that it became a game for us. We would count his utterances of *dear God*, and after the first few times hearing him, we made a game of it. Using a betting analogy, we basically had an under and over for how many times Brother Simon would say *dear God* in his prayers. So once the preacher called on him, we did our own little dear God preprayer to the Brother Simon prayer.

"Please, dear God, let this prayer be shorter than his usual ones because we are awfully hungry, and the food is getting cold."

"Brother Simon, please lead us in prayer and bless our food on this wonderful day," Brother Applegate requested to every church member's favorite Deacon and elder. The silliness and pettiness of us boys making fun of his prayers and creating a silly game of counting his *dear Gods* was not intended as disrespect but just young boys being immature and silly. Everything else about the man presented a different picture.

Brother Simon was very tall, and even in these later years of his life was the most imposing individual in our entire congregation. To those who did not know the man you would undoubtedly be intimated by his stature and countenance. I never once saw the man smile or laugh but his presence exuded reverence and created a feeling of goodness, security, safety and the list of positive adjectives to describe how he made you feel is endless. Thinking of Brother Simon I am reminded of the older gentlemen in the movie *"Home Alone"* played by Roberts Blossom. Kevin was initially terrified of Blossom's character Old Man Marly and his snow shovel, but Old Man Marly turns out to be a wonderful man who saves Kevin from the Wet Bandits, Harry and Marv. In my mind the two men Brother Simon and Old Man Marly had to be related and are friends upstairs looking down on us from above.

Brother Simon assumed his standing prayer position. Standing tall and erect in front of the congregation with his long arms meeting at his waist with one hand clasped over the other, he closed his eyes, slightly bowed his head and began to pray.

"Dear God, thank you for this wonderful day, dear God and dear God, please be with us here, dear God, as we worship you, dear God, and, dear God, help those in need, dear God, as we, dear God, once again, dear God, are blessed to serve you, dear God. And, dear God, thank you for all the wonderful ladies, dear God, who prepared this food, dear God, and dear God, bless this food to the nourishment of our bodies. Amen," Brother Simon concluded, and slowly raising his bowed head I watched him as he ever so slightly turned his head and seemed to be focused on a specific part of the congregation.

What is he looking at, who is he looking at, I thought to myself? This time there was not an over and under and counting of *Dear Gods,* but I had listened to the words and content of Brother Simon's prayer and his message. The combination of our visitors, the reaction of certain members of the congregation to their appearance and now Brother Simon holding center stage was riveting theater for a young inquisitive boy and had increased my attentiveness to my surroundings. I then realized what Brother Simon was doing. His stare was focused on the part of the congregation where our visitors were. Without saying a word, he paused and with a squint of his eyes and tightening of his face, he scowled at the very same ladies who had scowled at our visitors.

I am thinking to myself *yes, one scowl deserves another, git em Brother Simon,* as I tried to contain my excitement with a fist pump towards the ground but wanting to raise my forearm and fist pump for all to see especially the old scornful women, yet then again there was the momma eyes on me from the choir factor, so I controlled my excitement. Brother Simon then ever so slightly began moving his head more towards his left and while looking at the two men who had come to break bread with us the look on his face changed. No longer a scowl but a modest smile and with a slight bow of his head he said to the two men, *Welcome.*

I am not sure if others witnessed this exchange, but I am sure of one thing, I did. And I know for certain the scornful old ladies felt it, the young men felt it, and God for sure took notice.

I think back to those times and for me that was when Brother Simon received his admission to heaven. If there was ever a man with a free pass to heaven, it would be Brother Simon. I would envision the meeting at the pearly gates going down something like this.

"Name please," Saint Peter would request.

"Brother Simon," he would rely.

"Dear God, it's the dear God one himself. Go on through, Brother Simon, you have nothing to prove here," Saint Peter. would say.

Well, the food was delicious and as usual we all had a great time.

Once we finished up and were headed home, us boys had more questions than usual.

"Daddy, how come those two guys came into the church instead of just getting the food that was there for the taking? That's the only reason they showed up anyway," Brad asked.

"I'm not sure, son, but hats off to them for joining us in the service. It was the Christian thing to do to feed these men, as it appears they were down on their luck and hungry," replied Daddy.

"How come some of the ladies were making bad faces at those men?" Brad continued.

"Well, obviously, they forgot last week's sermon where Brother Applegate quoted Matthew chapter 7. Judge not that ye be not judged. Obviously, those ladies were looking through dirty windows," Momma jumped in.

"Momma, what do you mean by looking through dirty windas? How do you know they have dirty windas, Momma?" "Have you seen their windas? Bruce asked her.

"It's an expression. What it means is best explained by a story. There was this young couple eating breakfast one sunny morning, and through their dining room window, they observed in the yard next to them their neighbor hanging her laundry," answered Momma.

"Won't you look at that woman. She sure does not know how to wash her clothes properly. Look how dirty those sheets are," the wife said disgustingly with disdain.

Her husband just shook his head and made no comment. This went on for a few days, with the wife always commenting on her neighbor's dirty laundry. Finally, one morning, she was in for a big revelation.

"Well, well, color me surprised. She finally learned how to properly wash her clothes. Wonder what happened?" the wife asked.

"Here is what happened, honey, her clothes were never dirty; I washed our window," the husband replied.

Finishing her little story, which Momma did often to explain things, she would always then put the ball in our court.

"So, what does that story teach you?" asked Momma.

"Those who live in glass houses should not be throwing stones," said Brad.

"Dirty windows, glass houses, what does all this mean?" asked Bruce.

"What it means, son, is that before finding fault in others, focus on being the best person you can possibly be. Those who continuously find fault in others may discover when taking a hard look at themselves they are not so perfect. Many times, those who find disdain for certain traits of others are often guilty of and possess those same negative characteristics themselves. And whether intentionally or unknowingly, they project these same perceived shortcomings and negativity onto others. Either way, it is the wrong thing to do. Again, according to the good book, 'Judge not, that ye not be judged,'" answered Momma.

"Momma, we were taught in Sunday school that Jesus loved the little children, all the children in the world, Red and Yellow, Black and White; they are precious in his sight. Does it still count if they are grown up and are dirty and smell bad?" I asked.

"That's right, son, and yes, regardless of if they smell bad or look funny, Jesus still loves them. And being grown up does not matter as well. We are all, regardless of age, God's children. Under this beautiful sky and heaven, we are all one family, just different. Those two men, along with everyone, are God's children as well," Momma acknowledged.

"I have a tough question. Is church a building or is it the people?" Brad proposed.

"The answer is yes, but it takes a very special building to be a church with the right people to be a church. And on top of that, it is the presence of God in combination with those two things that make a church. I think you need those three to have a church. If we would have treated those men badly and forced them out, then I would argue that a piece of God would have left with them. At some point, you would end up with a building of hypocrites, not a church, as opposed to a house of the Lord," answered Momma.

"Daddy, how come those men dress like they do and look so different?" Bruce wondered.

"I got this, Dolph," said Momma. "Well, son, they could ask the same question about us. It's all about choice, and being different is just that. Two people being different does not always equate to being right or wrong. Two people can be totally different in how they dress, how they look, how they talk, and there is no right or wrong to be assigned on either part of that equation. It's just a matter of individual perspective."

"What is purspectiv?" Bruce pondered.

"Perspective is how you see things. You may look at these men and think they are on the road, hungry, unsettled, and needing assistance from time to time. They may look at themselves as having freedom of movement, exploring the country, and every day a challenge and adventure combined with meeting new people. They made the choice to live that way, and if they are causing no harm to anyone, God be with them, and the least we can do as Christians is to put some warm food in their belly and send them off better than when they met us," explained Momma.

Changing the subject "I think Bobby has a new purspectiv," Bruce announced.

"Really?" smiled Momma.

"Yeah, I think he has a girlfriend," replied Bruce.

"I do not, what are you talking about?" I replied giving little brother the big brother stare down.

Yes, you do. I saw you and that Gina Stafford girl talking when we was at Vacation Bible School. And when we was playing Red Rover, you kept runnin her direction, right into her arms," exclaimed an animated Bruce spreading his arms as if in the actual game.

"It's part of the game, dummy," I said.

"Yeah, but why every time you went that way, and you both kept callin each other over and over by name and also you was holdin hands, so she is your girlfriend," confirmed Bruce.

"No, she ain't, she is jus a friend," I piped.

"She's a girl, ain't she?" asked Bruce.

"Yes, she's a girl," Duh, I muttered.

"And she's your friend, so she must be your girlfriend,"

I said nothing. Painted into a corner by my little brother, I decided to stop digging.

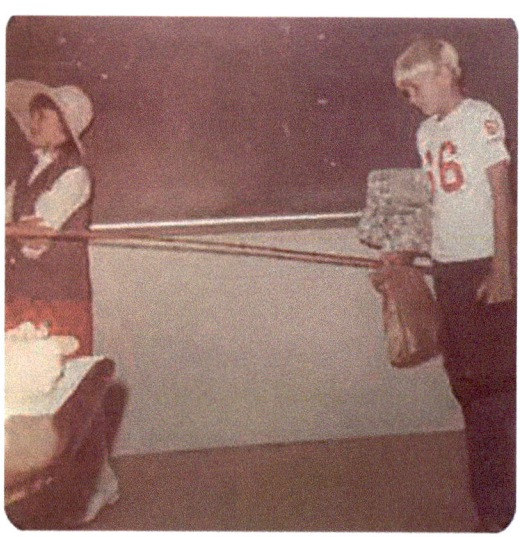

Charlie and Josephine, me and Gina Stafford in our acting debut at Arkansas State.

I had no comeback, and besides, I did like Gina. She was smart and pretty like Skillet, but unlike Skillet, she really was sugar and spice and everything nice. Skillet, like boys, was made of snips and snails and puppy-dogs' tails, and on top of that, she was mean.

A few years later, me and Gina would be the main actors in a play Momma wrote, and made our acting debut in Jonesboro, Arkansas, at the Arkansas State University. Cousin Chet and little brother Bruce had bit parts, but me and Gina were the stars of the show, Charlie and Josephine.

What a day that was. Strange visitors showing up at church and me being outed by my brother for having a girlfriend and likely to be kicked out of the esteemed He-Man Woman-Haters Club. Lots of revelations on that Sunday. As for the two men, Dad told me later that some of the men took up a collection of money for these two gentlemen and wished them well. Thinking back, if you cannot go to a church in time of need, where can you go? And isn't church a good place to meet a girl?

Momma was an angel that day. I learned more from her in ten minutes than a lifetime of preaching would ever provide. It had a special meaning coming from my mother to me. After many years in the army and traveling to different countries all over this world, Momma's words would over and over ring true and could be taken as gospel. I encountered all types of people in all types of places like Chad, Tanzania, Russia, Israel, and Egypt, just to name a few, and what I discovered was that people are pretty much the same wherever you go. Every country and every race have good people and some bad people.

There was always lots of singing in the church

"In the Sweet By and By (We Shall Meet on That Beautiful Shore)," "Old Rugged Cross," "Amazing Grace," "Onward Christian Soldiers," and "Just as I Am." All these songs have amazing stories behind them. "Amazing Grace," probably the most famous, was written by John Newton. The life story of this man is nothing short of fascinating. My favorite was "Onward Christian Soldiers" which the hymn's theme is taken from 2 Timothy 2:3. "Thou therefore endure hardness, as a good soldier of Jesus Christ."

Momma was always singing around the house, so it stands to reason she would sing in the choir. She was part of a quartet with Edward Barger, Charles Davis, and Evelyn Smith, and they were very good. Every Christmas, the choir would have a Christmas cantata, and Dad would tape it. The most memorable recording one year was the thud of little Wally Dial's head when he slipped and fell on the pew. I'm sure even the man upstairs got a chuckle out of that one.

Food

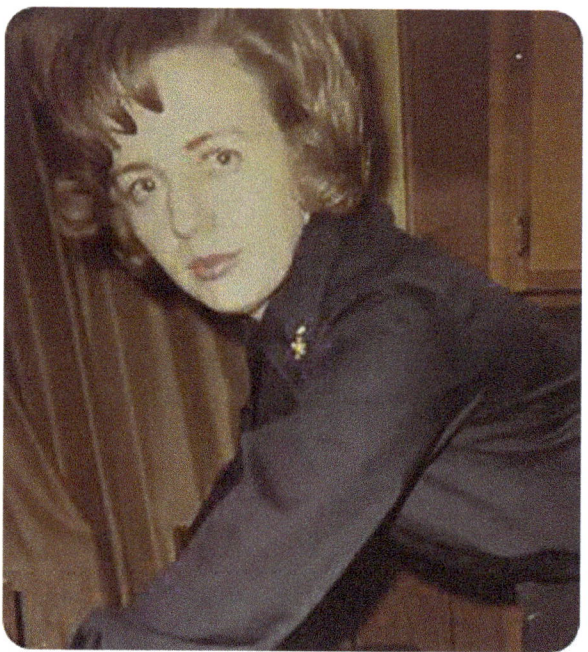

Beautiful Momma serving up a dish.

Momma was a great cook. Being the oldest girl in her family, she learned at an early age cooking and cleaning and helping to raise her younger siblings. Like most Southern women, she had mastered the art of frying chicken. But her most delicious dish had to be her roast and potatoes and carrots for Sunday lunch. She would put her pot on a slow burn just before we went to church, and it would be just about ready when we returned home from Sunday sermon. Speaking of the sermon, I can remember we boys always sat in the back of the congregation, and Momma in the choir up behind the preacher could watch us like a hawk. Afterward, she would always critique our behavior on how well behaved or not we were during the sermon. Instead of being proud that Momma was one of the best singers in the choir, I had a negative outlook. I thought it was unfair that my momma could see me during the sermon, but other kids with no parents in the choir got a free pass. A thirty-minute sermon may not seem like a long time, but to a kid, who to be honest really wasn't that interested in what the preacher had to say, it could seem like an eternity.

"Bobby, I saw you back there just squirming like a worm. Can't you sit up straight just for once and at least pretend like you are paying attention to what Brother Applegate has to say?" said Momma.

"Momma, I really am trying, but he keeps telling the same stories over and over, and to be honest, some of what he has to say, I find it a little hard to believe," I insisted.

"Do tell," said Momma.

"Well, like dat story about dat guy named Jonah. Now how can a whale, which I learnt in science class has a small throat, swallow a man whole? And he sat inside dat whale for three days. What was he doing in there? And what on earth is he talking about it being easier for a camel to go through the eye of a needle than for a rich man to enter the kingdom of God. Everyone knows ain't no camel small enuff or needle eye big enuff for that to ever happen. Ain't none of us gittin in so why waste my time listenin to such nonsense. And while on the subject, you tell me why Noah didn't jus smack those two skeeters dead? We got so many of those dang thangs flying around they might as well be the Arkansas state bird,".

"Someday you will understand. Just have faith. "Some things are to be taken literally and some figuratively," said Momma.

A few weeks later, it was my turn to be the critic. One must be careful by the rules they set since they find themselves having to live by those same rules made even more difficult when on public display for all to see. Brother Applegate had gone over his allotted time, and I seemed to notice that this time, it was Momma, oh so very slightly, showing some concern on her face and, shall I dare say, doing just a tad bit of fidgeting. It was my turn to observe and take notes. It seemed like she was trying to relay some type of signal to my dad with little repeated head movements upward and to the right (later, this was translated to mean "Quick, go get to the car; we are in a hurry to get home). Dad apparently understood what Momma was saying, because immediately after the sermon, he quickly assembled us boys, rushed us to the car, and was waiting on Momma. I had never seen Momma in such a hurry and move that fast as she ran to the car in her Sunday best, having even pulled off her high heels. She jumped in the car and told Dad, "Quick, get home."

"Momma, what in the tarnation are you doin?" "Why are we in such a hurry? And I noticed you up there just squirming away like a worm up there in the choir. I thought you told me to always sit up straight and still." I told her.

"You got me, son; now how do you want your roast, burnt on one side along with the house on fire?" Momma asked.

Momma always timed it perfectly to arrive home just in time to flip her roast so it would not burn on one side. This time an extra-long sermon had pushed the envelope, and Momma wasn't one to waste food.

Well, I thought to myself, *mommas are human too. I am sure God would understand.*

If there was one thing, I remember Brother Applegate always said, it was that God was very forgiving, and if he could forgive Momma for squirming, then he surely could forgive me, but it was Momma I had to satisfy on that front.

Bacon grease

If you ever looked under our sink, you would see a jar of goo, and if you didn't know what it was, you would never guess. Momma would occasionally take a spoon of this horrible-looking stuff and add it to green beans or some other dish she was cooking. How could something that looked that bad make something as plain as green beans taste so good? Easy. After cooking up a mess of bacon in the morning, Momma would take the remaining grease from the frying pan and pour it into a jar where once it cooled, would just be a glob of goo to be used in numerous recipes as delicious seasoning.

While talking about bacon, when did this other pretend bacon come on board? What the heck is turkey bacon? Should there be allowed such a thing? Seems a little on the sacrilegious side of things when it comes to an acceptable breakfast staple. Personally, I would crawl through broken glass for real bacon, second only to Arkansas round steak, bologna. Whether uncooked with crackers or even better when fried and on a sandwich with Miracle Whip, bologna, like bacon, is heaven-sent.

The only real bacon is the kind of bacon that comes from a pig. I would think that pigs had a monopoly or some type of copyright on the word bacon not to be confused with that wannabe fowl and foul prototype, turkey bacon. Stand down, you gobbling impostor, you may rule the roost in November for Thanksgiving, and even some refer to it as Turkey Day, but that is once a year. In my book, every day is Bacon Day.

Chapter 3

BIG PHIL AND THE GANG, OUR SPORTS COMPLEX, DEER FISHING, FLORIDA BALL, AND THE REDBIRDS

The Spicer and Williams boys, me, as usual, into something.

Our little group of giants on Woodlawn would become the best of friends. For us Williams boys, it initially began with our immediate neighbors, Mark and Ricky Spicer. It then expanded to other kids on the street to include the Suttons and the other Spicer family. From that group of boys, it would be Big Phil Spicer that would emerge as the patriarch of our gang. His little brother was Rodney, but there was nothing little about Rod. He was also taller and bigger than most kids his age and, like his brother, an excellent athlete. They had a little sister, Leah, but unfortunately, she was outnumbered as most kids on our street were boys. The Busbys, David known as man who jumped off cliff and his big brother Tony. The Williams, myself, and my older brother, Brad, and younger brother, Bruce. The other Spicers, Mark and Ricky. The Suttons, Steve and Doug. The Musicks, Doug and Jimmy. The Weston family, James, Tim, and Jimmy, and lastly, Bill Drennan, Gary Wilburn, and the Stevens, with Ricky and Marty and Pam and Brenda. Later, some new girls moved in—Janice, known as Skillet, and her sister, Sylvia, but we were too busy doing boy stuff to worry about girls, and besides, girls had cooties.

So those were the Woodlawn families. There were other kids, but they came from other streets and might as well been from different countries. We liked them okay; they were just not part of our gang, the Woodlawn Giants. The only admission to our gang was either you lived on the street, or you were family, like Perry White and Keith Dial who did eventually end up living with us for a short time. We liked those fellas on Gathings and would sometimes associate with them. I can remember the Maness family, Tim, Jimmy, and Danny, and the McFerrin family, with Mike and Mark. They were all great guys, and later, after graduating from high school, it would be Tim and I who would be roommates all the way out in California, imagine that.

The parents, our own sports complex, and the hood

Mrs. Mary Jane Spicer, a second mother to me and many others on Woodlawn. It truly takes a village.

One of the things I remember most back then was that if you were misbehaving, other parents would not hesitate to put a bee in your britches. A close-knit group of God-fearing Americans with an "it takes a village" mentality meant you were hard-pressed to go unnoticed. There were proxy parents everywhere, and it was an acceptable practice. They were there to administer adult supervision in the event your own parents were not present or in the immediate vicinity. Mrs. Mary Jane Spicer would not think twice of putting me in my right place, and Mrs. Geneva Joyce Williams had absolutely no problem with that as well, whether it be Ricky from the Spicer family or one of the Sutton boys or anyone for that matter. In one case, it was Mark and Brad that threw lots of mud bombs and dirt clods on the Sutton's carport (this was before the Suttons moved in). Mr. Rick Spicer didn't wait for Mr. Adolph Williams to get home and ask for permission to punish the two culprits. He had Brad and Mark over there atoning for their crime and doing a massive cleanup operation. Let the punishment fit the crime, and we soon learned. There was more than one set of parents' eyes watching over us, and that was a good thing; we needed extra supervision.

Mr. Rick Spicer, him and Dad were the nicest two men you ever met and best of friends.

Mark and Ricky's daddy, Mr. Rick Spicer, had to be one of the nicest men I ever knew. The time he would spend on the backyards to ensure us boys had fields to play all our sports on will always be remembered and cherished. When Mr. Rick finished one of his projects, right away you would notice his attention to detail. Long before *Field of Dreams*, it was Mr. Rick who got out the lawnmower and bags of flour and built us a baseball field on the church lot behind our backyards. Apparently, there were no issues at all for us to use this property, and that was a blessing. Complete with a state-of-the-art backstop, he also provided us with an infield by cutting the grass, complete with tiered base paths. Kids from all over would come just to play sandlot baseball. We were truly in high cotton and thought that baseball field was the cat's meow, and of course, we were professional ball players because if the "Amazin' Mets" of '69 could win it all and be champions, then so could we.

It was only Big Phil and Mark who would routinely go yard and park homers on the church roof to dead center. Back then, what seemed like massive shots on the church that seemed so far away shrink in distance when I revisit now. Funny as a kid what appeared huge, to include swings on playgrounds, appears to shrink in size as you get older. I wonder how many baseballs landed on that roof. The church had a unique construction with two separate wings, a blocked letter *U* shape with the connecting portion of the building facing East Barton and the two wings extending back toward our properties. This created an alleyway between the two wings and occasionally a line drive straight shot to dead center would end up between the wings.

Shows the gap between wings of the church where Big Phil lined it deep center and Vic got close to God retrieving it.

One such Big Phil homerun shot reminiscent of Mark McGuire's record breaker; a low line drive ended with the baseball stuck in a vent. Vic Butler, the center fielder, rushed in the alleyway and quickly climbed up to retrieve the baseball and perhaps still make a play at the plate. As usual, Big Phil was taking his time to leisurely round the base path, and if Vic could retrieve the ball in time, there was still a chance to make a play at the plate on Philly. Only one small problem. Who in their right mind stuck playing catcher would be willing to block home plate with Big Phil charging down the line, not me? Getting bowled over by Big Phil at home would have made the Pete Rose and Ray Fosse collision pale in comparison. Afterward, when talking about that Big Phil's line drive between the wings and Vic trying to retrieve it, it was Danny Straubie who said that was the closest Vic had ever been to a church in his life.

Long balls were not the only distance records owned by Big Phil. We would make competitions out of everything. One of them was who could toss a 45 record the farthest. Winner again, Big Phil, with a toss from his front yard all the way down to Ricky Steven's house. That is a record that stands to this day mainly because the 45 has become an antique and collectible item. People aren't winging them just for fun. Anyway, I digress back to Mr. Rick, our groundskeeper.

In addition to the baseball field, Mr. Rick and Dad built us a football field spread out over our two backyards. Again, out came a bag of flour, and we had a field complete with yard lines. Remember the pines. It was the pines that were just outside of one of the sidelines. I remember one play where Mark was the lead blocker on an end around, and for a second, Steve thought he could get through Mark and make a play on the end running with the football which was little Bru headed toward the end zone. Mistake. The result was Steve becoming airborne and flying over the top of those pine trees. As some of the boys like Big Phil, Rod, and Mark got bigger and stronger, we had to adjust the rules because they were impossible to tackle. It would be a hybrid of touch and tackle where all we had to do was two-hand touch the bigger boys, and tackle was still on for the rest. There was still some peril in that construct in that Big Phil, Rod, and Mark could still tackle you.

But these boys were aware of their strength, and clocking someone was not the intent. We were there to have fun, so when a small, skinny guy came head-to-head with one of those three, they would simply pick you up entirely off the ground and let you down easily.

Daddy on the job at Sears.

Running in parallel with Mr. Rick was my father, Adolph, known as Totsy. Like Mr. Rick, another one of the kindest men I have ever known in my life. If there was a competition between Mr. Rick and Mr. Totsy as to who was the nicest man on the planet, it would have been a co-MVP year. What a tandem. It was no wonder that Daddy and Mr. Rick were like peas in a pod and were the best of friends. Both were excellent fly fishermen and, with their popping bugs, would just wear out schools of bream on Horseshoe, Bear Creek, and Wapanocca Lake. Whenever Dad and Mr. Rick would return from their fishing trips, we would run out to see the catch of the day. One day, we were in for a big surprise. One of the fish was the biggest fish I had ever seen them catch, and it had antlers as well. Okay, it wasn't a fish. It was a six-point buck, a deer in the trunk of that red Chevy Impala. How it got there, how two guys fishing came back with a deer is another story for another day. Let's just say they didn't catch it on a popping bug. A few weeks later, we were at the Razorback barber shop getting our buzz cuts, and I was chatting away about how my daddy went fishing and caught a deer.

"Hop up on this booster, son, and let me give you your haircut. Same way as last time?" Mr. Bill asked.

"Yes, sir," I answered.

"What have you been up to lately?" asked Mr. Bill.

"Not much, but my daddy and Mr. Rick went fishing and caught a deer."

"A deer? You mean a fish as big as a deer, or a real deer?" asked Mr. Bill.

"I mean a real deer. He had horns too."

One small problem on that day was there was a game warden present whose ears perked up when hearing that, but Momma put him at ease, saying, "Bill, you know boys will be boys, and this one can spin some yarns. He gets it honestly from his aunt Pat, my sister, who just fills his head with all sorts of crazy things. Last week, he came home and was telling me about a pie factory across the bridge. Well, we all know that building is the sewage treatment plant. And who would believe that? After all, how many people go fly fishing and catch a deer?"

Momma then gave me that look, and I realized story time was done, sat quietly, got my buzz, and stepped down. Shine gave me one of those suckers with the looped fiber handle as a reward. I then proceeded silently and nervously sucking my sucker back to my seat in a chair right next to Momma who patted that spot as a signal for me to sit down and shut up. I knew that face.

Back to sports. Daddy built us a full court basketball in the backyard. We played outside so much that the grass in the back had zero chance of growing. The yard was solid dirt and packed so hard on that Arkansas gumbo that it rivaled any concrete or wooden court. A dribbler on our court would most likely have less bad bounces than a dribbler would have in Boston Garden. Later, Dad would add another goal, allowing us to play full court.

More football

Is there anything like backyard football? That was probably the sport we played the most. Later, both Mark and Big Phil got bigger and stronger, and their long passes would cover the entire length of our original field in the backyard. We then expanded our operation and switched to playing our games in the church lot, with the slope leading down to the bayou as one sideline and the wall of the church extending with an imaginary line as the other sideline. But in the beginning, it was our backyard combined with the backyard of the Spicer's as our field. Our field, just like the old NFL fields where the goal post began at the end zone, had obstacles as well. We had to negotiate the basketball hoop which was an eight-by-eight beam support that Dad had cemented into the ground. It was quite the obstacle, and if defending, you had to be careful that the receiver didn't run you straight into it, thus freeing himself up for a wide-open reception. Our style was a more wide-open offense, much like the Canadian Football League, and since we had no indicators to ascertain when the offense gained ten yards for a first down (the flour did not last long), we devised our own system of keeping the drive alive for the offense. That would be three completions in a series of four downs which made for some interesting fourth-down decisions.

Knowing that the defense would crowd the O-line to defend against short completions, Mark and Big Phil drew up plays to counter that. I can still remember the huddles where the QB with a twig would scratch out a play in the dirt and, with very rudimentary *Xs* and *Os*, tell us where to go. One of my favorites was the button hook, but the most exciting play is if you were chosen to be one of two flankers in a crossing route and headed downfield to opposite sides of the end zone for a Big Phil or Mark long ball, simply called a bomb. Both QBs had the art of pump-faking to one receiver and then turning and launching to the other receiver. Catching a long ball from Phil or Mark made your day. Another play was the Statue of Liberty where the QB, resembling the pose of the Statue of Liberty, with one hand in the air and the other hand at his side, would just stand there and hand it off to an end coming around for an end around. It was on one of these where Mark as a lead blocker sent Steve flying over the pines.

What I remember most about these games was how the bigger boys would play down a level to include the smaller kids. Big Phil having to reach way down on a Statue of Liberty play to hand off to little Bruce and then have Big Phil lead the blocking meant Bruce would get some glory as well. The seas pretty much parted on defense when Big Phil was leading the charge, and whoever was running behind him was in for a big gain. I can remember one time he picked up Bruce and carried him and the ball over the goal line for a touchdown. Long before there was Karl from *Sling Blade* being nice to someone smaller and letting them score in a pickup football game, there was Big Phil. I just thought that was so special and cool, and looking back, it seems even more awesome and a testament to what awesome kids were on that street. These big guys on the block, Mark, Rod, and Big Phil were true gentle giants.

Big Phil and Brad on the Woodlawn Diamond that Mr. Rick built.

So, there you see we had a big three: football, basketball, and baseball sports complex in our own backyards, courtesy of our fathers. Dad also helped us as we sponsored the neighborhood Olympics. What wonderful things fathers can do for their children with so little.

Florida Ball and more on Big Phil

Every year when the Spicer (Phil and Rod) family would return from Florida, they would bring numerous balls of different colors that were something between hard plastic and rubber. These soon became the balls used in the Spicer's backyard for baseball games that came to be known as Florida Ball. Here is where the goodness and benevolence of the gentle giant Big Phil was on full display. Once Big Phil determined he dominated every single sports game in the neighborhood, he looked for ways to allow smaller kids more opportunities to play. What a nice and unselfish gesture to share the spotlight with smaller or less talented kids to make them feel special and included.

Another way the bigger boys would get the smaller kids involved would be letting them be their designated base runners before they got on base. It was Big Phil and Mark and sometimes Rod who were the ones who routinely parked long balls on the church. Big Phil, after multiple homeruns and trips around the basepaths, would ask one of us little kids if we wanted to run for him. You would then line up on the right side of the plate, and once Big Phil hit the ball into play, the designated runner would take off for first. If it was a homer, and many times it was, us little guys would run around the bases as if it was us personally who hit the homerun ball. Once, when retrieving one of Big Phil's long dingers, it couldn't be located. It was finally located in the front parking lot, in a trash can. So back to Florida Ball.

Big Phil did not play. Likely because the balls after he hit them would wind up in the Mississippi or even Memphis, Tennessee, but the real reason was more benevolent. Big Phil was our all-time umpire and statistician. Sitting behind home plate in his favorite lawn chair with what would be a modern-day equivalent of a Big Gulp, a large cup of ice water, and his scorecard, he would call balls and strikes. At the same time, he would also keep score and our personal stat sheet of RBIs, homers, base hits, walks, and strikeouts, the full gambit.

Again, way before there was Karl from *Sling Blade*, when Karl let the boy score, we had Big Phil. Steve, T-bone, had a wicked curve and none of us little guys could touch it. After multiple *K*s for us little guys and our apparent frustration at continuous whiffing Big Phil acted. In typical Karl fashion, he shrunk the strike zone for these strikeout kings, adjusting it so there were more walks, base on balls, and we were able to reach first. That may have made the pitchers angry, but Big Phil didn't care. As the Jim Croce song went, "You don't tug on Superman's cape / you don't spit into the wind / you don't pull the mask off that old Lone Ranger / and you don't mess around with Phil." Ball four was ball four. As for us little guys, it made us love him that much more.

One-time, little brother Rod drew the ire of his big brother, and Big Phil granted him a head start to run back in the house. Rod darted and weaved and thought he was home free as he approached the door, only to be beaned in the head by Big Phil throwing a basketball like it was a baseball. But that was just one case of boys being boys. These were isolated incidents. Mostly, we always got along, and most of the scraps were between siblings and your typical big brother little brother skirmish. I don't remember many of the disagreements, what I do remember is all of us getting along and just the best of times. One of the things that really stays in my memory is when one of us had the wind knocked out of him and the sight of Big Phil standing over him. Placing the kid on his back, Big Phil would grab the injured party by his waistband and gently lift him up and down, calming him down and, in the process, allowing him to get his breath back. I can still see that.

Professional sports

We were all huge sports fans, and there were no professional teams close by, and this was well before the Oilers moved from Houston to become the Tennessee Titans. While on that subject, don't you think they should have been named the Nashville Cats?

Remember that name? That would have been much cooler and fitting in my book. And should not a team name have something to do with the geographical region from which they play? There are no grizzlies in Memphis but some on Vancouver Island; there are lots of lakes in Minnesota, not so many in Los Angeles; and I am certain there's not a lot of jazz in Utah, everyone knows the Big Easy is the birthplace of jazz. See where I am going with this, sports fans? The closest I ever remember to a professional sports franchise to getting this right had to be the Memphis TAMs as a member of the American Basketball Association, ABA from 1972/73. Can any tri-state fans tell me what a TAM was, or what TAM stood for? The answer is in the question—TAM stood for Tennessee, Arkansas, and Mississippi. And did you know who the owner was? Charles Finley. Yes, the same Mr. Finley who was owner of the World Series champion Oakland A's. Was this team the TAMs any good? No. I really believe some college fellas named Finch, Robinson, and Kenon would have beaten the TAMs. But back to our beloved Redbirds, our Cardinals.

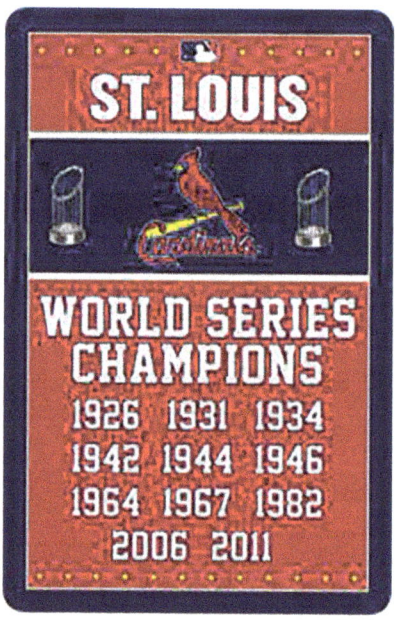

Five rings in my lifetime. Keep em coming Redbirds.

Cardinals Baseball

We loved the Saint Louis Cardinals. And if you were a ring counter then the number one reason would be the descendants of the Gas House Gang were winners. To date, they have won eleven World Series championships, second to the hated New York Yankees. One of those titles was in 1967 when they beat the Boston Red Sox and the following year, 1968, they were back in the series but lost to the Detroit Tigers. Even the teachers at school loved the Cardinals. Brad told me how at Maddux, they ushered all the kids into the cafeteria with TVs set up to watch the games. What cool teachers, I thought to myself. It doesn't get more American than baseball, hot-dogs, apple pies, and Chevrolet. Back then, there was no such thing as prime time requiring all the games to be played at night. There would be day games for the World Series. I guess the teachers at Dabbs, where I went to elementary school, were not as cool as the Maddux teachers, or maybe they weren't Cardinal fans. That meant in 1968, when I was eight years old, I had to sneak in a small transistor radio with a small earphone and try and listen to it in class.

My most fond memory of Cardinal baseball was when my uncle Bobby Dial, Pat Pat's husband, and father to my cousins Keith, Kris, and Kurt, drove me, Brad, Bruce, and Keith all the way up to St. Louis to catch a Cardinals game. Being able to watch Bob Gibson pitch a shutout against the Cincinnati Reds was just icing on the cake for four boys who were seeing their first professional baseball game. These were the same Reds that would go on to become the Big Red Machine a few years later. Thanks, Uncle Bobby Dial, for taking us there. If unable to attend a game or watch one on TV, we had radio. It was around 1972 that Mike Shannon, a former Cardinal, would join the radio booth and, for almost thirty years, was partners with Jack Buck, father of Joe Buck, partner to Troy Aikman on Fox Sports Network. We couldn't get enough of Cardinal baseball and to this day remain fans. Road trips up to Busch Stadium would continue, and eventually, what was measured by miles became measured by the amount of beer consumed. On one ill-fated journey, we never made it to St. Louis, and it would be Rusty and Luap to the rescue as Bruce's car broke down somewhere in Missouri.

Football Cardinals

Cardinal football was a tougher sell. The former Chicago Cardinals became the St. Louis Cardinals in 1960. Different professional franchises like football and baseball teams had shared the same name, but this was unique in that they already had the name; they just switched cities. In the sixties, when we first started following the Cardinals, they weren't very good. We still loved them though, and our Cardinal football heroes were Larry Wilson, Jim Hart, Roger Wehrli, Jackie Smith, and Jim Bakken. It wouldn't be until 1973 and the arrival of Don "Air" Coryell and new names like Dan Dierdorf, Conrad "Dirty Dobler" Terry Metcalf, and Mel Gray provided us an exciting brand of football and some playoff games.

So whatever season might be in full swing, or maybe a key game would fire us up. Immediately after the game ended, we would be running outside to play and emulate our heroes and replay a game. How many shots we had to take as the imaginary clock was winding down to hit the game winning shot. We spent most of our time outside because that is where the gang would be, and we enjoyed being with our friends. Just looking at our backyard, it was obvious by the lack of grass and packed-down dirt we spent hours upon hours there. Things with kids today seem to have taken a 180. When I was in trouble, the punishment was I had to stay in and was not allowed to go outside and play. It seems the exact opposite now.

Before:

Momma after me doing something stupid.

"Get your tail *in* your room. You are not allowed to go outside and play," Momma would always say.

Nowadays:

Kid gets in trouble.

"Get your tail *out of* your room, you are not allowed to remain indoors and play Xbox," modern day Momma might say.

Chapter 4

PARENTS MAKE MISTAKES TOO

Why there are professional moving services

Momma wanted a piano and was able to find one for sale from across town. Buying it was the easy part. Getting it from point A to point B was a challenge. So Daddy went to his go-to guy, Mr. Rick, and these two decided they would just get it into the back of a truck and haul it themselves. Piece of cake. What could possibly go wrong?

*Hanging out on our future planning spot,
L-R Bobby, Mark, Brad and Ricky, 1963. Years later we*

Me and Ricky were sitting on his front doorstep with Mark and Brad, one of our favorite places to hang out and swap stories.

"Momma is getting a piano," I proudly announced.

"How is it getting here?" asked Ricky.

"Our daddies are gonna deliver it," answered Brad.

"How they gonna do that?" asked Mark.

"Easy peasy, fellas, those two can do anything. If they can catch a deer fishing, haulin a piano ain't nothin. I saw em headed out in the truck. Let's go to the corner and wait for em. They should be here soon, they left thirty minutes ago. Wait, I wanna grab my walkie-talkies," I said.

We all headed toward Hamilton, and it was obvious we were up to something. Other kids asked what was up and when told of the big delivery, asked if they could tag along. Soon we had a small crowd gathered there at the corner of Hamilton and Woodlawn to greet our delivery men. Of course, I embellished the story as usual.

Momma is getting a grand piano, and my daddy and Mr. Rick, like professional movers, are deliverin it. They gots quilts, boards with rollers, ropes, and everything."

"I hope they move stuff better than you make jumps on your bicycle," taunted Skillet.

"Can't you ever let that be? This is a special moment. Mommas getting a piano, and with her singin and playin, she is gonna be in a band. Doug, do me a favor, take this walkie-talkie and go down to Barton and let us know when they are comin." I ordered.

"I'll do it, but I'm gonna need sumthin to eat for all that work," grumbled Doug.

"Okay, here is sum jerky from that deer Daddy and Mr. Rick got from fishin, er I mean huntin," I replied.

All the gang was in position, and the anticipated arrival was soon to become a special moment, in fact a little extra special.

Daddy and Mr. Rick were almost there. After successfully loading up the piano and transporting the piano all the way across town, they were almost home.

Turning right from Barton onto Hamilton, they saw Doug and, further down, what looked like a large group of kids hanging out at the corner.

"Rick, is that that youngest Sutton boy, Doug, sitting out here by himself with a walkie-talkie? And what are all those kids doing on the corner?" asked Dad.

"Beats me, Totsy, if he is a lookout he isn't a good one because his walkie-talkie is on the ground, and he seems focused on just eating. We're almost home. Let's wrap this up. Wait a second, why are all our sons with their friends on this corner? There is your middle boy with a walkie-talkie, which explains Doug. It seems they have formed up some sort of reception party," said Mr. Rick. (As the lead cheerleader, I had all the kids waving and cheering as they rounded the corner.)

After a successful transport under difficult conditions from all away cross town in a standard, three-on-the-tree stick shift and no power steering, they were making the final turn onto Hamilton for the final stretch. I was so proud and leading the cheers from our little crowd as they turned the corner.

"See, I told ya, Skillet. They were professional movers, look at em go. Look at dat piano. Momma is gonna be so happy!" I happily exclaimed and thinking to myself I finally was gonna show Skillet and Half-Pint that we Willams were more than just mistake-prone and unfortunate Woodlawners. Look at all the improvements with the help of Mr. Rick Spicer we had done for the neighborhood. We built a sports complex, entertained with events like the bayou jump and although there were a few accidents along the way we added much value to the Woodlawn Clan. One of my proudest moments.

My Daddy and Mr. Rick were now in the Red Zone approaching the goal line for a major score.

And then it happened. One, two, three.

1. Someone's dog ran into the street in front of the truck as Dad was turning the corner.
2. Dad hit the brakes.
3. Momma's "grand piano" lurched forward and then tipped over the side, crashing onto the street.

Daddy stopped the truck, and he and Mr. Rick got out obviously embarrassed at their bad misfortune.

"Well, boys, help us clean up this mess. We got some work to do," Daddy told us.

We helped Daddy and Mr. Rick pick up the pieces and get the mangled piano on the truck. They then finished delivering Momma her "grand piano."

I looked over at Skillet expecting a snarky comment. She always did at times like this. But she didn't say a word. Although most times full of snark she was also more than capable of switching gears and becoming a thoughtful and considerate loving person. This was one of those times as she silently mouthed to me *"It will be okay"*. She even helped in the clean-up operation.

Momma's "grand piano," all busted up and not looking very grand, then went into surgery. Not sure what was funnier that day. Was it seeing that piano fall out of the truck and the look on Mr. Rick's and Daddy's faces, or watching those two trying to put Humpty Dumpty, the piano, back together again? Looking back, I am sure both Mr. Rick and Dad appreciated that I had provided them with an audience.

A bunk bed and a report card

Mr. Rick and Dad built for me and Bruce the coolest bunk beds two brothers could ever wish for. How to describe? The bottom bed extended at right angle from the top, and next to it was a storage closet underneath the top bed, extending down to the floor. I think of that room and that bed, and the memories come back.

Each night, my mother would bring us a glass of water and say a good-night prayer.

Momma said, "Now repeat after me."
Now I lay me down to sleep,
I pray the Lord my soul to keep,
If I should die before I wake,
I pray the Lord my soul to take".

I never told Momma that her little prayer kept me awake all night, afraid to go to sleep.

What I really remember about that bed was something even more traumatic.

Remember back in the day how we could alter our report card letters, change an *F* to a *B*. Those days are gone as technology combined with smart phones and progress reports via email keep me posted on my kid's grades. Of course, when you were my older brother, Brad, you didn't have to change anything—all *A*'s as usual. Thanks, bro, for setting the bar so low—not. Report card day came, and somehow, Brad's perfect report card came up missing. And as always, I, as the usual suspect, was the first to take blame. Of course, why would someone who had all *A*'s on his report card lose it?

"Brad, bring me your report card," instructed Momma.

"I can't find it; last I saw, Bobby had it," said Brad.

"Bobby, bring me your brother's report card," Momma replied with the tone of her voice changing to more serious mode.

"I don't have it." I cried.

Interrogation commences as I am the one who must answer for the lost report card.

"Son where is the report card?" Momma barked, becoming more agitated.

"I swear, Momma, I don't know where it is."

As the interrogation continued, I got more and more worn down. I really understand how people can confess to crimes they did not commit because I would have confessed to anything to end my mother putting me through the ringer.

Finally, I was willing to cop a plea, and Momma helped me with my story.

"Listen closely, here is what happened. You were jealous of your brother's report card, correct?" asked Momma. (Looking back, that couldn't have been true because my grades were always good as well. If anyone may have been jealous, it would have been little bro Bruce, but he didn't care either.)

Just wanting it to end, I said, "Yes, Momma, I was jealous."

"You took that report card and tore it up into lots of little pieces and flushed it down the commode," said Momma.

"Yes, Momma, I took that report card, tore it up, and flushed it down the commode."

"Now you know, son, I'm going to have to spank you," said Momma.

"Yes, Momma." (to myself, thank God, this is now almost over).

I took my spanking, undeserved I might add, and I thought that was the end of it.

But it wasn't. Years later, when me and Bruce outgrew those beds, Daddy tore them out. Guess what had been hiding all those years behind the beloved bunk bed between the bed and the wall—Brad's report card.

That was one undeserved whipping from Momma, but I am sure there were many that were well-deserved that I escaped along the way. So, I was still in the red as far as getting over and away with things I should have gotten a spanking for, so I was good to go in my book.

Chapter 5

NASA COMES TO TOWN, BASKETBALLS, PIE, AND A TORNADO

Next Apollo mission for NASA coming to West Memphis

Boy was I on the receiving end of all jokes, which I think motivated me to be such a prankster later in life. The three most memorable were the ones that Steve and my aunt Patsy and her son, my cousin Keith, pulled on me. Starting with Steve. When they were first building the West Memphis water tower on our end of town, a young gullible boy would have never known by the initial construction phases what they were building. In the beginning, what I saw being built could have been anything. It's not like they haul a prefabricated complete tower to a predestined location, prop it up, and it's done. What was it? One day, my curiosity got the best of me, and I asked Steve. That was my first mistake.

"T-bone, what are they building over there next to the fire station?"

"Can you promise to keep a secret? You cannot tell anyone.

Only a few people know about this. It will be our secret," whispered Steve.

"Cross my heart and hope to die, stick a needle in my eye," I swore.

"This is top secret information. Can you believe how lucky we are? Our town has been chosen by NASA as the next launching pad for the next Apollo mission. They decided to launch a new rocket ship and are building it right next to the fire station in case there is an emergency. Move over, Cape Canaveral, it's our turn!" boasted Steve.

"Man, dat is sumthin. How long will it take to build? I questioned.

"It's gotta be quick. We are in a race with those Commies to see who can be first on the moon," answered Steve.

"Yeah, I learnt in science class dat those Russians made a Sputnik, and since then, we were in a space race. I hope we win."

"You may hear some talk that it's going to be a water tower. Don't believe it. The authorities putting that out there so the truth doesn't get out to the public," Steve elaborated.

I felt so special being privy to such a big secret, and ole T-bone just strung me along and played me like a fiddle. Finally, in the final stages, something seemed off to me. When the actual tank was attached to the top of the structure, it looked nothing like any rocket ship I had ever seen. One day, I cornered Steve and asked about this.

"Steve, that sure doesn't look like any rocket ship to me. It is starting to look like a water tower." I contested.

"Cobb, that is all part of the deception plan. Soon they will remove that portion, attach a space capsule, and launch," claimed Steve.

NASA comes to West Memphis, dang T-Bone.

I ended up getting strung along another few months on that whopper. I finally realized after they began painting it and reading about an upcoming mission in Florida, I had been had. They finished painting that red tower white, and it still stands to this day with the West Memphis Blue Devil logo painted on the side.

Basketballs

Aunt Pat the Prankster, I learned from the best.

Aunt Patsy and cousin Keith, Kris, and Kurt lived in Memphis. Whenever I visited, they would pick me up in West Memphis, and we would head to Tennessee. Once crossing the bridge, we would take the I-55 exit and head south toward their house on Dearborn. That route provided two targets of opportunities for my gullible mind. Firstly, was the Old Bridge itself. As we passed over it, Pat Pat questioned me, "Bobby, did you ever wonder how those bridge supports can withstand all this weight from these cars and big trucks crossing over this bridge?"

"I never really thought about it," I replied.

"Each bridge support has a basketball in the center that binds all that concrete together. Sort of like a keystone locking everything in position," Pat Pat divulged what she had learned in her Engineering class at Tyronza High School.

It sounded logical to me, but why a basketball and not a football? I left it at that.

A pie factory

As we took that first exit south off the Old Bridge just after coming into Memphis, target number two presented itself. A raw sewage factory.

"Isn't that a lovely smell? Breathe deep, son. Those are fresh pastries and pies. We are passing a pie factory," said Pat Pat.

I took some deep breaths and sniffed as hard as I could. It smelled like what it was, but I played along and just let it be. Cousin Keith just sat there with a grin on his face, knowing I had been had again.

Revenge

Revenge is a dish better served cold and the last laugh sometimes requires time, to properly set up and you must wait for the perfect moment.

Fast-forward twenty years later, and West Memphis had a terrible tornado. I was living with my brother Bruce at the time, and we were right smack center of the path of the storm over on Julia Street.

Once it passed, we were glad to be alive. Concerned about our parents living a few streets over on Wilson, we then procceded to make our way over to check on them. As we reached the corner of Julia and McAuley, we ran into Harold Patterson, a family friend who lived next door to our parents, driving his car. He informed us that their houses were fine, they were not even in the path of the storm. Later we found out our parents slept through the entire storm.

Pulling up right behind Harold in another car was my cousin Keith. Cousin Keith (remember the pies and basketball) had driven over from Memphis to check on the family. Keith parked off to the side, and we then reentered Julia, which was a complete mess. Across the street from Bruce's house, the only thing that remained of three houses were the foundations. The tornado had jumped over Bruce's house, lifting the roof about three inches and causing other damage. My car was totaled, and there was stuff all over the place. It really did look like a war zone. Me, Bruce, and Keith started working our way back down Julia, and across the street a few houses down, we ran into an ambulance. Apparently, there was an injured woman, and the first responders were in the process of a medical evacuation. The fire department personnel asked us to assist in clearing a pathway from her house to the ambulance, and of course, we were obliged to do just that.

The next day, I decided that a prank was in order. *What an opportunity*, I thought to myself. A chance to prank my cousin, and operation payback kicked into high gear. I guess I learned from the best, Aunt Pat Pat. I waited for a few days and then called my cousin Keith and told him that the *Evening Times* (our local newspaper) had got word of our heroic rescue of the injured lady and wanted to do a cover story, but they needed a typed-up account of events.

Keith bit hook, line and sinker and typed up the sappiest account you could ever dream of.

It went something like this:

> As I was driving around Memphis, I heard on the radio of the tornado hitting West Memphis. I then, out of fear for my loved ones, drove as fast as I could across the bridge to see if they were okay. I ran into my cousins who having survived the perilous storm were making their way through the war-torn neighborhood looking for survivors. After dodging downed power lines and gas fires, we heard a horrible scream. It was a woman buried under massive rubble and debris, and me and my cousins sprang into action, removing the debris and clearing a path for transporting the poor injured lady to the curb while we waited for an ambulance. If not for our heroic actions, she would have surely died.
>
> Larry Keith Dial, aka LKD

This is good' I told him, an awesome account of events and that I would turn his work over to the *Evening Times*, and surely it would be published.

The hook was set, now to reel it in a little at a time. Every week, he would call me and ask what the status of the story was and when it was going to be published in the paper. I would string him along with replies that the paper was doing some editing, and it would be out soon. He finally got impatient and said he would talk to the front office therefore I let him off the hook.

"Hey, what gives? When is the story going to be published?" Keith was demanding an answer.

"Hey, cuz, remember those pies and those basketballs?"

"I will be bouncing those basketballs and eating those pies when your story gets printed,'

I am still waiting for payback, but in my book, in our own version of tag, he is still it. He can try, but I ain't gonna fall for it!

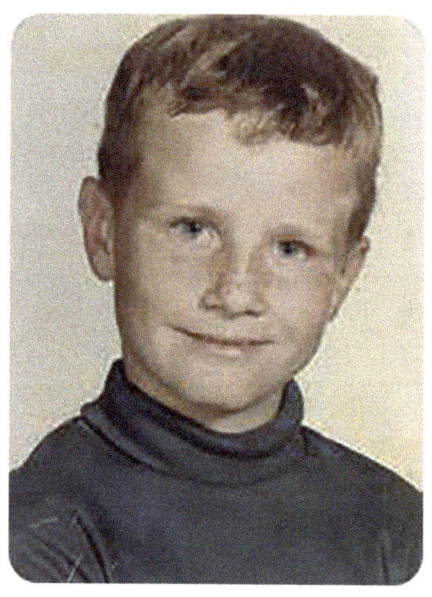

LKD, my cuz and prankster, pies and basketballs, tag you are it cuz, tornado hero.

Chapter 6

BAYOUS, BAR PITS, AND CUTOFFS

Ten-Mile Bayou

Our love of water and fishing began with something nearby, the ten-mile bayou. Me and Ricky Spicer lived on that thing. Every contraption or way to catch critters, we figured it out. One was using bacon on a hook to catch crawdads. How these crustaceans could be so stupid to hang on to that piece of bacon as we pulled them out of the water toward captivity was unknown to us. Apparently, their cousins, the Bluewater crabs in Ocean City, Maryland, are not much smarter. Fifty years later, I was using the same technique to haul crabs out of the bay using raw pieces of chicken. Catching those crabs with chicken made me think, *I've been here before, albeit it a little different.* I also remembered running into Ricky years later and laughing about catching them crawdads on the bayou using bacon.

Momma and Mrs. Mary Jane found out we were pinching slabs of bacon to catch crawdads. Let's just say we were strongly encouraged to stop using bacon and come up with other methods of catching critters. What we came up with, with help from our fathers was our new favorite, the rake. The rake was basically a long pole, and attached on one end was a wire mesh rectangle open on one side facing back toward the user. One would toss the contraption out toward the middle and then quickly drag it across the bottom. Once on shore, you would dig through the muck and goo and find various critters to include turtles, crawdads, tadpoles, and sometimes snakes. You had to be careful with snapping turtles because if they bit you, then according to legend, they would not let go until the next sound of thunder. So, the closest to a storm you could deal with them, the better. Oh, the silly things we do because of ridiculous wives' tales.

Other adventures on the bayou were frog gigging. Mr. Rick, Dad, and Uncle Larry would go out on a Friday night, and by the next morning, you would wake up to a bucket full of frogs, and once the legs were cooked up, they did not taste like chicken; they tasted like frogs. The technique involved head lamps and a long cane pole with a three-pronged spear on the end. As nighttime came, you could hear the chorus of the bullfrogs bellowing as Dad, Mr. Rick, and Uncle Larry boarded their jon boat and made their way down the waterway. As they progressed, the choir would be diminished one member at a time. The light from the men's headlamps would locate a frog, that frog would freeze in place and then one of the three men would add a frog to the tally with a sharp thrust from the gig.

I am sure PETA would not approve of frog gigging. Probably discussing over a chicken dinner or a hamburger how those hillbillies down in Arkansas were spearing frogs with primitive gigs and eating them.

Bar pit

From the bayou, we progressed to bar pits. Whenever inter-states were built, the engineers and road construction crew would excavate gravel and soil to create roadbeds. Later these man-made holes fill up with water and become ponds or even small lakes. Not sure how fish found their way into these American-made bathtubs, but they did. My memory of these brings back one of the most extraordinary names on our street Mr. Greenberry Squire Weston. If ever there was a name competition on our street for unique first names, either him or my dad, Adolph (no middle name) Williams, or Horace Drennan would be the top three competing for first prize.

Anyway, one Saturday morning, I must have been super bored because I was kicking an empty soft drink can down the street, and Mr. Weston, observing from his house, took notice and came outside and asked me if I wanted to go fishing with him. We had a great day, and I had one of the many thrills that comes from fishing when I caught a grinnel. What's a grinnel, you ask? Think of a prehistoric fish known as a bowfin. An ancient fish that swam in the same waters that dinosaurs stomped through. I caught a five-pounder that day, what a thrill—more fun than kicking a can. I am sure that was not in Mr. Weston's plans for the day to take some kid from down the street fishing, but he did. What a kind gesture on his part. Up to that point, I had minimal contact with that man. It just confirms just how special our neighborhood was in that he took time out of his day to entertain me.

Thank you, Mr. Greenberry Squire Weston, what a true gentleman. A squire in my book. Maybe not an attendant so much to a young lady but kind enough to be an attendant to a bored young kid. Kind enough on a Saturday morning to take time out of his personal schedule to spend time with me and make a special memory.

Oxbows, cutoffs

But by far the most exciting when it came to bodies of water would be cutoffs. What's a cutoff, you ask? A lake that used to be part of a river. Another special thing about West Memphis is it is a short distance from the Mighty Mississippi, the fourth longest river in the world. As a river grows in age, it starts to meander more and more, and eventually, cutoffs are formed. They are known as oxbow lakes (remains of the bend in the river), formed when the main part of a river has cut across the narrow end of the bow and no longer flows around the loop of the bend. It is erosion that creates a new channel to be cut through the small piece of land at the narrow end of a meander with the river making a shortcut, leaving a still water lake behind. The closest one to us would have been Dacus Lake. Other ones we fished further away in Arkansas were Horseshoe Lake, and in Mississippi was Tunica. These cutoffs were high adventure, and we devised all types of ways to catch our number one target, the catfish. But catfish were not the only critters in the dark murky waters. There were gars (basically alligators without legs, a fish), loggerhead turtles of enormous size, freshwater eel, and the most feared was the dreaded cottonmouth. A species of pit viper that is the only venomous species of North American water snakes. The last thing you want to encounter on a dark night out on the lake is a cottonmouth. They could be anywhere. Once, one fell from a tree branch into the boat as we were crossing underneath. At night, your head was on a swivel, looking for no-shoulder Jake.

Trot lining

A simple and cheap way to catch lots of catfish was a trot line. One of the best things my father ever taught me. The first step was getting bait. That required a decision on whether to use live bait or frozen shrimp which came in a box and was sold at the Red Barn on Broadway. To get the live bait, all you needed was a bucket to house your crawdads once pulling them in with a crawdad rake. The crawdad rake was the same one I explained in my bayou escapades. Pull them in, throw them in a bucket, add some water, and you were set. The smaller crawdads made for better bait because they had smaller claws and were less menacing than the larger ones. Crawdads were also good bait because they would live on the hook for several days at a time. Fish can be finicky, so to determine what they may be eating you would alternate hooks, baiting them with both crawdads and shrimp.

Now you are in your boat, a jon boat (flat-bottomed boats were perfect allowing you to get into tight spots), and ready to catch some fish. If by yourself, and many times I was, just sitting at the front with a paddle sculling made for easy and efficient maneuver. Setting up the lines was a simple process. Just having a roll of nylon line and either securing it from one tree to another, running it horizontally along the shore, or attaching to a tree close to the bank and running your line perpendicular to the shore out toward the middle and tying off with a brick and letting it sink to the bottom.

For the lines running horizontally to the shoreline, I would go from tree to tree or stump, whatever was there. After securing the beginning of the trotline to a tree, sometimes the branch of a tree if possible, I would then work the line out and tie off a loop with an overhand knot and then paddle toward my ending anchor point. I would not attach the hooks just yet to prevent entanglement. I would separate these loops by about a foot, and once reaching my far side anchor point, I would secure and in effect, depending on how long I wanted it to be, would have a line with anywhere from twenty to thirty loops on it.

I would then work my way back toward the middle of the line and tie a brick to weigh it down, keeping it securely underwater. After returning to the start point, I would then start attaching hooks to the loops but hold off on the bait. The last thing I wanted was a big fish getting caught, followed by a giant tug on the line, just as I was placing more hooks on the other loops (didn't want to be like brother Bruce with a hook through his finger). Once reaching the far side end point, I would then work my way back, baiting with crawdads by hooking them through their tail. My work was done; it was then a waiting game. We would check them once before leaving for the night, perhaps catching a few, returning home, and come back at the crack of dawn. Later when I started driving, I can remember checking my lines before going to school.

Returning early in the morning was always an awesome experience. The water would be super calm like glass, and many times, we would be the only ones on the lake. Nothing is more exciting as you approached your lines to see, if tied off to a willow branch, your line moving up and down of what had to be fish on the line. It was also fun to set lines in the farm fields next to the lake. Every year, the snow in the north of the country melts, and in early spring, the water from the main river reconnects with the lake. It then rises and flows over the normal shoreline back past the trees into the open farm fields. I can't tell you how many fish I caught in less than a few feet of water on land a few weeks later that would be tilled and prepared for spring planting. Once again, having a flat-bottomed jon boat was key for navigating these shallow waters.

Once retrieving my usual mess of fish, it was home and then the laborious process of cleaning catfish, a fish with skin as opposed to scales. It involved making a small hole underneath the fish just below the head and hanging the fish from a nail on a tree or post or side of a building. You would then make a small incision across the top of the fish, close to the head, and using the pliers, start pulling off the skin all the way past the tail. Bigger older fish had a tougher skin and were more difficult. It would then require cutting off the heads and making the necessary cuts to the headless body in order to remove the inside of the fish. After that, it was business as usual, and you cleaned the fish like you did all the others. You would then either fillet it or cut it into chunks, then rinse off the pieces of fish, and you were ready for a fish fry. If not eaten that day, we would pack them into empty milk cartons, fill them with water, and put them in the freezer.e.

My favorite trot line stories

1. Daddy's flashlight

Dad and I were out late one dark night, checking our lines. I was at the rear of the boat with Dad's beloved flashlight, and Dad was at the front, checking the lines. It happens to us all, and somehow, I dropped his light into the water. In complete darkness, I could sense he was looking at me and he said, "Well." "Well, what?" I replied.

"You know what must be done," Dad told me.

"No, sir, I do not," was my response.

"One of us must go in and get that light, and you are the one who dropped it," Dad added.

"You can't be serious, Daddy!" I exclaimed. (Me thinking to myself, *who in their right mind would go into this dark murky water home to snakes, snapping turtles, and whatever else in God's creation might be down there.*)

"Don't worry, son, I got this," chuckled Dad.

Dad then stripped down to his underwear, and off the boat he went. A few seconds later, he surfaced with his beloved light in hand, climbed back on the boat, got dressed, and, as we say in the military, we Charlie Miked, continued the mission. That had to be one of the most fearless or craziest things I had ever witnessed. My dad who was small in stature was a giant that night. That took some serious courage.

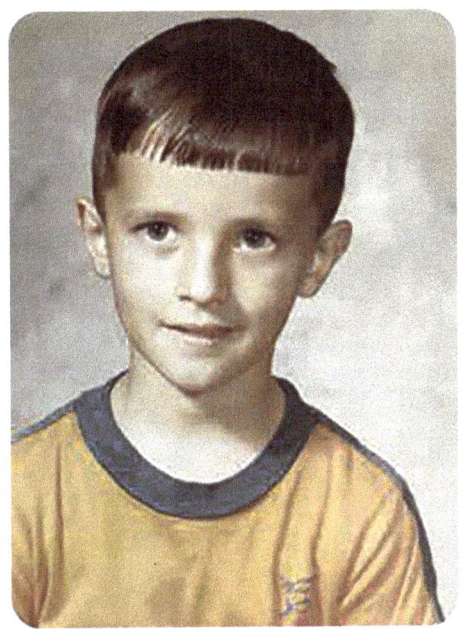

Little Bro Bru, sorry about the hook and eel.

2. An eel in the dark for Bruce

One morning, when checking the lines, there was about a two-foot freshwater eel on the line. I decided not to mess with it and just left it on the line to deal with it later. Later that day, the opportunity for a perfect prank entered my head. I thought I would take Bruce with me and give him a little scare. It was an especially dark night with little to nothing help from the moon. Normally, one always wanted to be the one who would take the fish off the line, and we would, as we always did to decide, do a quick rock, paper, scissors. The winner could choose either to be in the rear as the captain and controller of the small outboard motor of the ship, or the first mate. The first mate had the honors of sitting in the front and having all the fun taking the fish off the line.

It went down like this. One, two, three. I played paper, which covered Bruce's rock.

"Hey, Bru, you can have the honors. I'll run the motor and hold the light," I offered.

"Thanks. I need to stop going rock, you go paper every time," said Bru.

Laughing, I said "Well, that is because like a rock, you go rock every time. I got to warn you, bro. This morning, I was out here, and there were Jakes (snakes) all over the place. Looked like cottonmouths, must be mating or sumthing."

"I ain't afraid of snakes," boasted Bru.

"We will see about that," I murmured to myself.

"I have a good feeling we will catch a big one tonight. I found this cove I think is a good location," I told Bruce and was glad that he could not see the smirk on my face.

We then got to the cove, and the line that was attached to a small branch was just bending down as if a strong wind was blowing. It would go down and then jerk back up again over and over, just what you wanted to see when checking your lines.

Unknown to Bruce, this was the exact line that had the feisty eel on it, and I knew exactly where it was, about halfway down the line.

As we eased up to the line, Bru reached in with the paddle and raised it up to start working his way down to take off our catch.

"Man, there is something huge on this line. It is pulling hard," said Bru.

In the first few sets of hooks, Bru retrieved a relatively small catfish, about a two-pounder, but the line continued to jerk. I assisted, keeping light on the subject.

"Well, it isn't this fish, must be a bigger one down the line," little brother excitedly exclaimed.

After the first fish was off, safe in the cooler, I went into action. I shut off the light, and it was pitch dark.

"Sorry, bro, the light just went out, must be the rust on the terminals. Wanna wait till I get er fixed?" I asked.

"No need, I have done this so many times I could do it with my eyes closed," boasted Bru.

We were getting closer and closer to my eel or what Bruce thought was a big catfish.

"Bobby, it's a big one. He really is putting up a fight," shouted my little brother.

Just as Bruce got close to that eel, the eel wrapped itself around his arm, and Bru had the scare of his life. Of course, it's easy to confuse an eel with a snake, and I am sure that is what he thought was attacking him. He almost jumped out of the boat getting that eel off and himself away from that line. Had to be one of the funniest things I ever saw.

"Hey, the light seems to be working again. Go figure," I said. What are brothers for?

3. The other side of Tunica Lake

Myself, my grandfather, my uncle Larry, and his son, my cousin Scott, were fishing down at Tunica Lake in Mississippi. Uncle Larry was always so good to us, taking us fishing and hunting, and we always had a great time. I was about fifteen, and Scott was a small kid. Uncle Larry's friend who lived on the lake was a commercial fisherman, which meant he did it for a living, and naturally, it being his lake, he was the expert. It was early evening, and we were going out to set out lines with me and Scott in one boat and our competition, Uncle Larry and Mr. Expert, in another boat.

"Well, are you boys gonna set out your lines?" asked Uncle Larry.

"Uncle Larry, me and Scott are gonna cross over to the other side and set our lines in those trees over there," I pointed out.

"Son, why are you going all the way over there? There are plenty of fish right here. Just ask my friend, he knows this lake," insisted Uncle Larry.

"I believe you, Uncle Larry, but we want to cross over to the other side over by that clump of trees,".

"Go ahead, son. Good fishing,".

So, me and Scott crossed over and set up multiple short lines running between trees close to the shoreline in shallow water. This time we used minnows for bait, another good catfish catcher. We finished baiting up our lines, and when we returned later that night, we had a few, but when we returned early morning, it was a bonanza. Never have I caught more catfish in such a short time. We literally slayed them and returned with two coolers full of catfish and some really nice ones.

Big D, who was aware of the unofficial competition, was waiting down by the dock.

Just as we pulled up, Uncle Larry and the so-called professional Mr. Expert, the Bill Dance of catfishing, pulled in with their massive haul of two.

Final score: my Arkansas Razorbacks, me and Scott, twenty-two; Ole Miss Mr. Expert and Uncle Larry, two.

I don't know who was more proud or excited—me, Scott, or my grandfather.

That story has stood the test of time, and like the missing report card I always reminded my mother of, I would remind my uncle Larry that it was just fine to fish on the other side of the lake.

Yo-yos

Other methods we used were jugs, drop lines, and yo-yos. Yo-yos were a contraption, round like a yo-yo, that you would hang from tree limbs. We would paint them with fluorescent paint so that we could locate them easier in the dark. After securing the yo-yo, you would attach a hook and swivel to the end of the line and then pull out the length of line for how deep you wanted to fish. There was then a trigger that fit into a notch. Once a fish took the bait and was hooked and tried to swim away, it would pull the line away from that notch, and the yo-yo, by design, would start pulling upward, exerting a constant pull on the fish.

We would set out anywhere from a dozen to two dozen of these yoyos, and once in place, we would simply paddle a distance away toward the middle of the lake and look and listen using our spotlight to locate those fluorescent-painted yoyos that had been triggered. Whenever one was tripped, it would make a noise, sort of a screeching sound, as the device, in the process of being tripped, was now playing tug-of-war with a fish. The bigger the fish, the bigger the commotion. That yo-yo would do all the work as the fish would try and get away, but the constant pull would eventually tire out the fish, and you could then remove it from the line. I can remember finding large fish so worn out from the fight they were literally sleeping on top of the water. Unlike trotlines, you needed to stay with yo-yos. If you didn't, then smaller fish, having been tired out, would become easy prey for turtles and even snakes. Another reason was yo-yos were expensive, not to be left to unsavory characters who might steal them.

Jugs

Any kind of jug would do. Empty Clorox jug, milk jug, or anything that floated and had a handle that you could attach a line to. Like yo-yos, you needed to stay with a jug because it was obvious when a fish was on the line, as your jug would be dancing around the lake. If it was a really big fish, that jug would get pulled completely underwater before popping up in another location. We preferred trotlines because when rigged properly and concealed, trotlines were next to impossible to find; only you knew where they were. We might throw out a few jugs just for fun as we were tending to our lines, but that was it.

Drop lines

Drop lines were one of the first techniques we ever used because of its simplicity. Just hang a single line with a hook and small weight from the limb of a tree, bait it up, and you were in business. When we were smaller and first learning night fishing, this was the method we cut our teeth on. We spent many Friday nights at Horseshoe Lake with Keith, Bruce, Dad, and Mr. Jimmy Smith. Dad and Mr. Smith would go out far and set trotlines, and us little ones would have a few drop lines set up close to camp.

INJURIES IN THE NEIGHBORHOOD

Like any neighborhood, we had our share of skinned knees, bloody noses and lips, and so-called normal injuries, like those attributed to tackle football with no pads. Or the numerous bike crashes associated with racing and jumping ramps added to the total. But some of these injuries were freak accidents.

1. G.I. Joe needs a fort

Boys would be boys, and we were getting hurt all the time. As previously mentioned, it was Doug and I who seemed to be getting injured on a routine basis. One day, when we were only six years old, Ricky Spicer and I were playing out front with some G.I. Joes and decided their army men needed proper protection. They needed a fort.

"Let's build dem forts. What can we use?" asked Ricky.

"Let's use a brick. I can get one from the flower bed, and we can break it up and use it to build a wall," I answered.

"That's a good idea," Ricky replied.

So, us two boys got a brick but then ran into some problems. Neither one of us was strong enough to break the brick into smaller pieces. After several unsuccessful attempts to break the brick by throwing it in the air, we asked Mark, Ricky's older brother to help who being bigger and stronger, would be able to throw the brick high enough so that when it came back down, it would break.

"Okay, guys, watch this," warned Mark.

He then tossed the brick high into the air, and what goes up must come down, and down it came.

"Watch out!" cried Mark.

And like Big Phil's ball landing in the trash can, the brick also found its mark. Square on the head of yours truly, Bobby Williams.

It was a knockout blow, and of course, lots of blood and panic ensued, but it was the same Mrs. Mary Jane who would not hesitate to put a bee in my britches that saved the day and took charge and got me to the hospital. It truly does take a village.

One of the ironic things is that it was a baseball cap that prevented the falling brick from severely injuring me that day. Remember the old ball caps and the button they all had on top? The corner of the brick made contact on my head square on that button, thus softening the blow. According to the doc who stitched me up, that little button was a game changer and prevented even more serious injury. Not that stitches and a concussion weren't serious enough. Just like cars, they don't make hats like they used to.

> Moral of the story: Bricks are not made to be thrown in the air; they are to be stacked properly, and if in a flower bed, left there.

2. Neighborhood Olympics

My dad, Mr. Adolph, known to everyone as Mr. Totsy, had assisted us boys in setting up a backyard Olympics. We had all the field events, including the high jump, long jump, and a discus throw. The discus was a two-pound concrete weight used for dumbbells. During one of the discus tosses, you had the Musick brothers, Jimmy and Doug, on opposite ends. Why a group was standing opposite the group that was throwing is anyone's guess. And you guessed it—Jimmy made a toss, and it hit Doug square in the head. Another Woodlawn concussion.

Dad was there to take care of the accident, and all was good.

> Moral of the story: Don't have a discus event in backyard Olympics with the Musick brothers.

3. Practice casting

I got a new rod and reel for his birthday, complete with a tackle box and some fancy lures with treble hooks. There was also a rubber weight with an eyelet and no hooks that you could rig up and use for practice casting in the yard. My goal was to become just as proficient as Mr. Rick and Daddy who both with their fly-fishing rods and reels could place popping bugs repeatedly in the exact same spot where a school of bream were and proceed to hook these pan fish repeatedly.

One day, as I was practicing my casting, I thought to myself *Why not use a real lure and pretend to be a real fisherman*. So, I took off the practice lure and put on a real one, which was a replica of a minnow with two treble hooks front and back. Not a smart move. The lure, like the brick, the discus, and Big Phil's record length homer into the trash can, found its mark. This time, it was in the seat of my pants. Oh, what trouble I knew I was in store for, because I had been warned, do not use these lures for practice, that is what the rubber one with no hooks is for!

And now here I sat with a lure stuck in the seat of my pants, and not wanting to undress in front of the rest of the kids, especially Skillet, and simply remove the lure safely. I asked my little bro Bruce to help me get it out. As I was lying flat on my stomach, the operation began. What a predicament, getting heckled by Skillet and the gang and hoping Bruce could extract the lure from my britches before getting caught by Momma.

"Help me get this out or I am in for a whipping for sure," I begged Bruce.

"Okay, sit still, and I will get it out," Bruce stated with confidence.

Just then, I jerked, and one of the hooks on the lure went completely through one of little bro Bruce's fingers.

Bruce let out a primeval scream, "aaaaaayyyyyy!"

"What's the matter?" I asked.

More screaming, Bruce shouted, "aaaaaayyyyyyyyyyy!" The more I squirmed and tried to see what had happened looking over my shoulder, the more Bruce screamed.

"Be quiet, Momma will hear you. You want to get me in trouble?" I pleaded.

Bruce screamed even more.

Momma came out.

"What on earth is going on here? Dolph, get out here!" Momma shouted.

Daddy came out, assessed the situation, calmed everyone down, got some wire cutters, and cut the shank of the hook with the barb portion still protruding through Bruce's finger.

Later at the hospital, they just numbed up the finger and pulled the straight end of the cut hook through little bro Bruce's finger.

Back at the house, Momma dealt with me.

"Take those pants off right now," Momma ordered.

"I can't do that, there are girls here. Skillet will never let me live this down," I cried.

"Don't make me count to three, ONE," said Momma.

I then quickly took off my pants knowing the beatdown that came with the number THREE.

In the end, I was unable to dodge that well-deserved spanking. Thinking back, I don't know what was worse—having to take off my pants in front of a bunch of girls, especially Skillet, or the spanking I got from Momma.

Witty, snarky, and loud as those yellow pants she has on. Janice aka Skillet.

My oh my if it isn't Bobby Williams. Is that the same bike you crashed in the bayou? Where is that fancy lure you got caught in your britches? Maybe you can use it for a xtrey bike decoration. You still got hook holes in your underwear? What was you trying to do catch a fish on your butt? Who do you think you are, Bill Dance?" Skillet jeered laying it on thick.

Oh jeez, I thought to myself, now I got none other than Dr. Skillet and her tiny sidekick to deal with. And now it was Half-pint's turn.

"Every time you boys try something new; someone gets hurt. You almost killed my brother in your stupid Olympics! And who pretends that weights are a discus? I know who, someone who fishes on grass," Carla taunting me and answering her own question.

I felt like saying to her that it was her own two brothers' stupidity that created that incident. That everything was going perfectly until one brother took the other one out with an ill-advised and ill-timed toss. But I was in a hurry and didn't want to argue with these two.

Sticks and stones may break my bones, but words will never hurt me, Dr. Skillet and Half-Pint," I said while pedaling as fast as I could to escape these two.

"What was you trying to do, catch your little brother? You can't even catch a cold. You Williams boys catch funny things on your fishing trips, deer and people," Skillet hollered at me as I tried to escape their heckling.

"Yeah, that hook was all the way through his finger. That had to hurt. Remind me not to play with you, "shouted Carla.

"Don't worry about that, you two. I got much better things to do than play with cootie nests," I hollered back.

> Moral of the story: Listen to your parents when they tell you not to do something. There will most likely be consequences if you do not. At least there were when I was growing up.

4. A dead fish can hurt you

Dad and Mr. Rick would go trot lining at Bear Creek and come back with lots of catfish. In a cooler on our back porch, there was the catch of the night, and our dads had iced them down to clean later. We were not the only ones who wanted to see the fish, and with a group of kids gathered on the back porch, Mark wanted to show off the catch of the day. So, he reached to pick up a fish to show the other kids, and he got finned. The pectoral fins on a catfish are for their protection and are barbs with inside edges like a serrated saw blade. And just like Bruce was howling on the back porch the day he got a hook through his finger, Mark was howling up a storm, having been finned by what appeared to be a harmless catfish.

> Moral of the story: Again, listen to your parents. If they say don't play with the fish, don't play with the fish.

5. A hatchet, a porch, and Doug's head

We returned home one evening from a visit to my grandparents in Tyronza to discover a massive amount of blood on our back porch. Yes, our back porch again. Seems like it was becoming a cursed location. We had no idea where the blood came from. I was just glad it wasn't mine for a change. Unknown to us, Steve and Doug and some other kids were hanging around, and not sure how it happened, but Doug was chopped in the head by a hatchet. His new nickname became Hatch, short for Hatchet Head. Later I asked Steve how on earth Doug got hit in the head with a hatchet. What he told me had to be one of the craziest stories I have ever heard.

We knew you guys were out of town, and we were hanging around and playing Split the Kipper, "began Steve.

(Split the Kipper was a game that required soft ground, hard shoes, a knife, and large amounts of stupidity. It was a game of two people standing opposite from each other with their legs together. The first thrower of the knife aims and throws it, so it lands outside his opponent's feet. It must stick or be close to their feet or it doesn't count. If it does stick, then the opponent must slide his foot to the location where the knife successfully stuck. The game had different rules and variations and usually ended when you got bored, or someone ended up with a stuck foot).

"How did a game of Split the Kipper end up with a hatchet to Doug's head?" I asked.

"I'm getting there. We figured it might be cool to play something new like appleshot," explained Steve.

"What is apple-shot?" I asked.

"Remember when that guy William Tell shot the apple off his son's head?" asked Steve.

"Yeah, so what," I replied.

"Well, we found this hatchet laying on your back porch, and I thought we would play a new game with the hatchet except this time, we would throw at a pear on someone's head. I had Doug try and put one of your helmets on, but it was too small. Then after some practice throws, we really got good throwing that hatchet and decided I could throw a hatchet at Doug's head and knock off a pear," said Steve.

"Something tells me you missed, or should I say didn't miss," I laughed.

"Yeah, I didn't mean to of course, but I hit my brother in the head with a hatchet," admitted Steve.

Moral of the story: Don't play with hatchets.

6. Building a car

Steve, Doug, and I had decided to build a car from scratch. With two-thirds of this crew being the top two injury leaders on the block, the odds this endeavor would not end well were very high. The material consisted of scrap lumber, some old, discarded wagon wheels, ten penny nails, and a hammer and some rope. What could possibly go wrong? So, the boys got to building, and the result was the ricketiest contraption one had ever seen. The wheels had no tread and were attached loosely with ten penny nails that functioned as makeshift lugnuts. A rope was attached to the front for pulling.

Even by their low standards of safety and construction, this thing, not even deserving of a proper name, looked the worse for wear. Time to check it out and do a test run. This time it was rock, paper, scissors, and I won, or in retrospect, we should say lost, again as the first to ride in the car. Steve, being the bigger of the boys, was pulling, and Doug was pushing from the rear. I was perched in the driver's seat, and they started from the front of thier house headed toward the curve right there at the Windham's house. It did not take long for wheels with tread or rubber to become razor-sharp as metal grinded on concrete. As they were going around that curve to the right and centrifugal force kicked in, I was pushed to the outside of the curve, and put my left hand down on the street, and the back wheel partly spun and was dragged over my left forearm, and it was not a pretty sight. A nasty cut to my left forearm and once again loss of blood, this time in the street.

When Steve and Doug rushed me to my house, Momma was overcome to the point she nearly passed out from the sight of such a horrible cut and loss of blood. For once, it was helplessness and desperation that defined Momma's actions. I am not sure how this could have ended if not for our favorite neighbor, none other than Old Man D himself. The same individual we all hated and were constantly bad-mouthing. Thank God it was a Saturday and Mr. Donaldson was home and as usual working in his yard and accessible. He sprang into action and took charge applying a tourniquet to stop the bleeding on my badly cut arm. I received forty-five stitches that day on my skinny little arm.

It was a very serious injury, a cut severing the three tendons on my little, ring and middle finger on my left hand. The upper portions of the severed tendons had snapped back into the muscle on the arm. Dr. Jay had to make an incision to locate these detached tendons allowing him to pull them out and reconnect them to their respective counterparts thus allowing full use of those three digits. You may wonder how I could remember such details on the surgery. Because I had recently eaten, I was not put under for the procedure and watched him do his work. I even participated. As he would reconnect a tendon, he would tell me to move that finger to ensure the digits were functioning properly.

Every serious cut leaves in its wake a scar. This scar is unique in that it is in the shape of the letter "L" The long part of the scar is from the accident and the shorter part of the scar is from the incision Dr. Jay made to retrieve the three severed tendons. In addition to the scar to remind of that day is that the tendon for my ring finger was damaged more than its counterparts. The result is that finger does not fully straighten out and extends ever so slightly in a downward trajectory. *"How many stitches did you get?"* would always be the first question a kid would get when returning to the neighborhood Dr. Jay told me it would be easy to remember how many stitches I got—just think of Colt 45. I did not know if he was referring to the malt liquor or the pistol. Anyway, I survived with just a scar and bent ring finger on my left hand.

Me and my Grandfather Big D. This was the trip back home where I linked up with Mr. Donaldson, OMD.

How ironic that the man we all talked about negatively would be the one who saved my life that day. I am convinced if that man would have not been there, I could have bled out. His same routine that had him staying home and working in his yard on a Saturday, which we previously exploited to use against him, is the same routine that saved my life. Many years later, thirty-five to be exact, I was home on leave and visiting with my grandfather. He would always go to Coleman's on Missouri Street, where he would meet with his buddies for coffee and conversation. I tagged along on one of these trips, and Big D, Grandfather, introduced me to one of the gentlemen, a nice man named Tommy. After sharing some conversation, I realized that man was Tommy Donaldson, the same man many years ago who took care of me in a time of need and kept me from bleeding out from that horrible cut on my arm. I showed him the scar on my arm, still visible to this day, and thanked him for being there for me.

Thank you again, Mr. Donaldson. It took a village that day, and how lucky we all were to have you as a member of that village.

Later in life when I had my own yard and spent an exorbitant amount of time making it look nice, I thought back to what Momma said about judging and to never judge because the projections invariably are those you possess yourself. Either currently or you will at some point in the future.

Well, guess what, once again Momma was right. All that time I was giving Mr. Donaldson the business for paying so much attention to his grass look who is doing it now, yours truly. Tommy Donaldson was not a bad man, just a guy who loved his yard—nothing wrong with that.

> Moral of the story: Ensure there is tread on the tires when you build a go-cart, and don't fault a man for loving his yard.

7. A harmless old dinner bell

When I was going to school at Dabbs out in Hulbert, we had a field trip out to Looney's Farm. There was this dinner bell on top of a shed that I assume back in the day may have been used for ringing to signal to the workhands that it was time to come in for lunch, or that it was the end of the workday or whatever. What it wasn't intended for was for silly children to be pulling on the rope and ringing the bell. Well, there was an extra bell rung that day, and it was mine. Off the top of the shed, she was pulled, and a tumbling down she came. Once again, I was the winner, the proud recipient of having my bell rung literally by a huge bell falling off and hitting me square in the head. After a trip to the hospital and a concussion, I did not remember much of that incident. Sort of like when Mark Spicer hit me in the head with a brick in the G.I. Joe incident, all I remember was coming to with a bad headache.

> Lesson learned. Bells are for ringing, not for playing.

Chapter 8

JOBS

Cotton: In the summer and in the fall

• *Chopping cotton*

Brothers Brad, Bruce, and I and cousin Keith got our first real job in the cotton and soy bean fields. nsir sweetheart job. We would get paid a dollar an hour and room and board to stay the summer in Tyronza, Arkansas with their maternal grandparents, Big D and Momo, to chop cotton. Chopping cotton is sort of a misleading term. You are not actually chopping the cotton but chopping down the weeds in the cotton field, mostly the Johnson grass. Why was it called Johnson grass? Was it named after a Mr. Johnson? Whoever Mr. Johnson was, we came to dislike him immensely. One of the pranks we would play against each other was to go back and replant the fallen Johnson grass on a row one of the others was working on so that when Big D came out to inspect, that person would catch his wrath and that was an encounter you never wanted to happen.

I remember one time, Keith was taking an extended break and was nowhere to be found, and Big D showed up for his morning inspection. "Where is Keith?" he barked. We tried to cover for him and said that Keith was most likely taking a number two since he had complained of an upset stomach and was having the squirts from eating a cupcake.

Big D went stomping through the rows saying that when he found him, he was gonna open a shoe factory in his backside (not his exact words; his were a little more explicit). Anyway, off he went searching for Keith, and when he found him, all we saw was dust kicking up, and Keith was soon back on the job hoeing away.

> Lesson learned: Don't sleep on the job.

Anyone that has ever lived in Arkansas, especially in the eastern part of Arkansas, in the summer knows it gets hot as Hades. A scorching sun, combined with extremely high humidity, makes for a difficult work environment, especially for city kids not used to the rigors of that lifestyle. Because of the extreme temperatures, we would get up early, catch a quick breakfast, and out to the fields we would go. The plan was to get in about five hours in the morning and then break for lunch back at the house and then that dreaded return to the fields for the last couple of hours of an eight-hour work day. Do you know how hard it was to return to purgatory after lunch? We started trying to cheat the clock, literally. As it started getting close to noon, someone would distract Momo, and we would repeatedly move the second hand back until the time was always a quarter to noon. That stunt only worked once, and we all were docked a case quarter from our salary.

> Lesson learned: You can't cheat the clock; you will get caught.

- *The negotiation*

It was me that thought we were being underpaid. A dollar and hour and room and board did not amount to much, and I figured we should be paid for our efficiency and for the number of rows we were doing. My math had us potentially doubling our money and making two dollars an hour since we were doing close to two rows an hour. I cleared it with the fellas and prepared my speech. One hot afternoon, when Big D made his rounds, I approached him with the proposition.

"Big D, we are doing great work here, and I think we deserve a raise. We feel we should be paid for how many rows we are choppin. For every row we complete, you should pay us one dollar," I proposed.

"Son, that is a great idea. You are quite the negotiator. Shake on it," he instructed me extending his hand towards mine. At a time when handshakes really counted and mattered, I was on Cloud Nine. I had successfully sealed the deal and was feeling all proud of myself. I had really accomplished something. How the fellas would appreciate my great idea and pulling one over on Big D. What a genius I was at having pulled off such a great deal, I literally started skipping back and once back with the crew excitedly told the good news to Bruce, Brad, and Keith.

Just then, Big D spoke up, "Now assemble your crew, grab your hoes, and get in the back of the truck. Bobby has made a great deal for all of you."

We then got into the back of the pickup as ordered, and off we went to a field where if you stood at the front of a row, you could not see the other end. The rows in this field were four times as long as the previous field. After an hour of work, the grumbling started. Even those not so good at math figured that we had been had. At the end of the afternoon, when it was all said and done, and the new arrangement had us making twenty-five cents an hour, Big D came and picked us up and we went home. That was one beaten down and dejected crew that rode in the back of that Chevy truck. I was up front in the cab with Big D. Usually another of the crew would ride there as well but not this time. The fellas wanted nothing to do with me. So, there I sat, and Big D started questioning me.

"Wheel, (that was his nickname for me), what did the others think about the great deal you made?

"Well Big D, you know Bruce ain't too sharp on his figuring, and Keith the conniver would find a way to make his mark by walking faster and choppin less which you would have noticed. It was Brad, cause he is older and smarter than the other two, which aint saying much, immediately knew my deal stunk to high heaven," I mumbled.

Big D did not say anything but that grin on his face said it all.

"You boys look tired, and why so quiet and dejected?" asked Momo once we arrived back at the house.

"They are fine, just learned a good lesson. Isn't this food great? Boys, I have a proposition for you. I am willing to pay you a dollar an hour, room and board, just like old times," offered Big D.

We jumped on it.

> Lesson learned: It sucks to be the negotiator when the new deal is worse than the previous one. Also consider the second and third order effects of each action you take or decision you make.

• *Stomping cotton*

The jobs related to cotton would not end with those hot summer days. It would continue into the fall when it became harvest season. Big D would be driving the cotton picker around, and we boys would take turns riding with him in the cab. Once his cage was full of freshly picked cotton, he would drive up to strategically placed trailers where we would be on standby. He would then pull up alongside the trailer and dump the load of cotton into the trailer, and that is where our job began. We were responsible for stomping that cotton down as much as we possibly could. The objective was to pack it down so that Big D could get the maximum amount of cotton possible into each trailer, and that required us jumping up and down to pack it down as flat as possible. The benefit of all this was it required less trips to haul the harvested cotton to the gin. That saved Big D money, and that was good. For us, personally, we preferred stomping to chopping.

• *A paper route and a man who would not pay*

Bruce and I had a paper route delivering the *Memphis Press Scimitar*. We would fold those papers up and rain shine or snow deliver them papers always on time to our customers. At the end of each month, it would be collection time, and we would go around and receive the payments. There was always this one man who was always late in paying. Can you imagine how cheap and lame someone must have been to continuously keep stiffing two kids on a paper route. One day, our problem was solved. Big D overheard me badmouthing the guy and asked what the problem was. After explaining to Big D, the issue of this guy always paying us late and requiring multiple trips to get what in effect was our cut, he said "I got this," "Where does he live?" Both me and Bruce at the same time excitedly pointed across the street directly toward his house and off Big D went to do some of his own negotiating. Not sure what Big D said to that man, but he was never late again in paying us. In fact, he became one of our best tippers. Now that is what I call taking care of business. Thanks, Big D.

> Lesson learned for that guy: Don't stiff little kids who have a mean-tempered Irishman for a grandfather.

Anyway, those were great times, and I remember riding from Tyronza back to West Memphis in Brad's blue Chevy Nova with a three-on-a tree standard transmission (how many of you young ins know what that is?) We would leave out Friday afternoon listening to Jethro Tull's *"Aqualung"* ("leg hurting bad as he bends to pick a dog-end" dogend is British slang for a cigarette butt), *Yessongs* from Yes, and Steely Dan's *"Reelin' in the Years."* Let's just say those eight tracks got worn out on our return trips home. One landmark was Stuckey's on the south side of I-55. Once we saw that, we knew we were getting close to home only for the weekend to fly by, and back to the fields on Monday.

Chapter 9

MUSIC, MY FIRST CONCERT, LYNYRD SKYNYRD, RIVERSIDE SPEEDWAY, AND A SNIPE HUNT

Is there any better music than Southern Rock? It was a band from Jacksonville, Florida's Lynyrd Skynyrd that I first listened to. Is any band better than Skynyrd? I beg to differ. For cousin Keith, it was Black Oak Arkansas and *"Jim Dandy to the Rescue"* that was his favorite song and band. I first started hearing this rock and roll, as they called it, as Brad and Bobby Wilkerson, Wilk, were jamming to Zeppelin or whatever the latest tunes were popular at the time.

But me and Keith didn't fixate on just US bands. Keith turned me on to some British sound, Joe Cocker, the *Mad Dogs & Englishman* was his cup of tea. My favorite British band at the time was the Rolling Stones and the *Goats Head Soup* album. The song *"Angie"* made me think of a girl named Angie at school. Ever wonder how special a girl must feel to have her name in a song. Like Angie from the Stones, or Amie from Pure Prairie League, Amanda from Boston, or Lola from the Kinks. Wait, that's another story.

Well, it was 1974, and I had scored some Lynyrd Skynyrd tickets. Some band named Golden Earring was second billing, but all I cared about was seeing Skynyrd on what my first trip would be ever to the Mid-South Coliseum, Memphis, Tennessee, for some- thing other than Monday night wrestling. I would be going with Chuck Davis, my friend from church who I first met (if babies can meet) in the nursery of Ingram Boulevard Baptist Church where we were escaping the preacher's sermons.

Daddy, after dropping us off from the little Blue Nova, had a few words of caution and encouragement.

"Be careful, boys, and enjoy the concert. I'll pick you up right here after the show," he told us.

"Thanks, Dad. Let's go, Chuck. This is going to be great," I said

"Yes, these guys are going to be awesome," added Chuck.

And great and awesome it was. My all-time favorite band, and I remember it like it was yesterday. We got to our seats and settled in for what would be our first concert. The song I remember most was not *"Free Bird,"* which eventually would become a rock anthem, but instead the songs *"I Ain't the One"* with a one-two-three intro followed by a short drum solo, rhythm guitars, a whistle, and inject of lead guitar that just pulls you right into the song—a classic. Also *"Call Me the Breeze,"* with Billy Powell on the keyboards. Who was this guy's piano teacher? Was it the Killer, Jerry Lee Lewis, himself? Unreal. But *"Sweet Home Alabama,"*—Turn it up and take that, Neil Young—was the most memorable and to this day my favorite.

What a show. A new experience for us and what would become the motivation for another Skynyrd song from the *Street Survivors* album a few years later was a smell, and yes, we could smell it. As soon as the lights dimmed in the coliseum, we got our first whiff and noticed an odd aroma of you guessed it—*that smell*, wacky tobacky. The guy next to us offered a toke off his left-handed cigarette, and we politely declined; it would be only ice cream sandwiches for us that night. Fast-forward almost half a century later. Bringing in 2021 the other night, around the fire, I was jamming to you guessed it—Lynyrd Skynyrd. That is forty-seven years of following that band. You might say I am a loyal fan.

Just as I reeled Chuck in back in 1974 to go see Skynyrd, it was my neighbor Pep from California that I invited in 2020 to go see Skynyrd's last concert from Jacksonville, Florida, showing at the theater at the mall on the big screen in Springfield, Virginia. It was a much different atmosphere this time, but the music was great as ever. The only original member still playing in the band was Gary Rossington. Replacing Ronnie Van Zant on vocals was his brother Johnny. Many of those early members have passed, but the band lives on in infamy. In my opinion, it is still some of the best, most meaningful music ever performed and recorded. On the way, I gave Pep a crash course on Lynyrd Skynyrd, explaining some of the songs and lyrics, and it's fair to see he has a newfound appreciation for the band. No reefer at that concert, just popcorn and Coke and two older guys enjoying a great show on the big screen. The fact that I am still listening to this band shows just how real and great their sound was and still is. Thank you, Lynyrd Skynyrd, from a fan for life.

For you soon-to-be and for you old Skynyrd fans, a little quiz. What song from *Street Survivors* is written by Merle Haggard? Who recommended Steve Gaines to the band? Who was co-lead vocal on the song *"You Got That Right?"* Why was the fire and flames removed from the album cover of *"Street Survivors?"*

Saturday night and Riverside Speedway

Big D used to take me to the races at Riverside Speedway. Even if you weren't at the races, you could hear them from our house. A quarter mile dirt track of Arkansas gumbo with racing stock cars and my favorite driver, Hooker Hood, seeming to always win made for a great night. All things are relative, aren't they? A kid with Big D his grandfather watching stock car racing in West, Memphis, Arkansas, would be just as thrilled and excited as a kid in California watching cars race at Laguna Seca Raceway or a kid at the Daytona 500. I remember the stands for spectators were old wooden bleachers, and they were positioned so close to the track that as the cars would spin around that one turn, they would sling dirt clods onto the fans. After the racers were done, there would be that special treat of demolition derby. How awesome for a kid to watch racing cars with his grandfather, followed by all types of cars intentionally crashing into each other in the derby. I also remember meeting my first drunk at the races. There was this one man being loud and obnoxious and yelling all kinds of crazy things.

"Big D, what is wrong with that man?" I asked.

"He is on the sauce, son," answered Big D.

"What kind of sauce? He sure does smell funny. I never smelled a sauce like that, never heard of Budweiser sauce, and he just keeps eating sauce with no meat, bunch of those empty Budweiser cans are under the bleachers," I pointed out.

Laughing, Big D replied, "Budweiser sauce, son, it's made for drinking. Let him be, he is just blowing off steam."

The great snipe hunt

It was late afternoon, and Steve had gathered the gang in a special clubhouse we had built.

"Steve, why you got all those bags?" asked Bruce.

"Fellas, tonight we are going to go snipe hunting!" said Steve.

"Snipes, what are those?" I asked.

"They are a bird that comes out at night, but here is the kicker. They can't fly. Sort of like mini ostriches except they are native to these parts," answered Keith.

"Well, if they can't fly, they should be easy to catch," I pointed out.

"No, they are superfast, they can even outrun you. These things could outrun Roadrunner," Steve emphasized.

"I'm hungry," grumbled Doug.

"You're always hungry. Listen up, once we catch all these snipes, we will have plenty to eat," with a word of encouragement to his brother Doug.

"So how do you catch them?" was my question. With Steve and Keith promoting this I was already suspect.

"That's why I have these bags and these flashlights. We will split into two teams, a drive team and a catch team. The catch team, the lucky team, will position themselves with the burlap bags and flashlights, and the drive team will go out and make some noise, and those birds will commence to running for their lives. The lucky ones, the catch team, just must stand there with the flashlight inside the bag, do a proper snipe call, and those birds will run right into those bags. They just seem drawn to the light, much like bugs to a bug zapper at nighttime," explained Steve.

"So why do you call the catch team the lucky team?" I wondered.

"Because they have all the fun. Me and Steve are the ones that must do all the work and run around and rile these birds up and run them towards you. All you must do is stand there with that light in the bag and catch snipes.

Steve, I change my mind. I want to be on the catch team," Keith requested.

"No, that wouldn't be fair. Let these guys be on the catch team. You had all the fun last time," Steve ordered.

The sun had set, and dusk was upon us, and the great hunt was about to begin.

We started walking all the way past Barton into new territory. You could hear the traffic on I-55 as those eighteen-wheelers were motoring by.

"First things first, we need to build a fire and cook up some grub to eat before we go out," suggested Keith.

"That's good because I'm hungry," mumbled Doug.

"You are always hungry, Doug," Steve affirmed.

"What we eatin, hot dogs?" asked Doug.

"No hot dogs tonight. I got something special—porkchops," said Keith.

"Pork chops, how we gonna cook pork chops out here?" I asked my cousin Chef Boyardee Keith.

This kept getting sillier and stupider by the moment.

"You'll see," beamed Keith.

We then built a fire, set up our little base camp, and Keith started cooking. How did he do it? Well, he pulled out a fork and started grilling a pork chop. It worked. Maybe not the tastiest thing, but I didn't hear Doug complain.

After filling our tummies, we then went into a final planning session for the big hunt.

"Remember, fellas, like fishing, you got to be patient. Once me and Keith stir em up, it will take some time for these critters to find you. If you do the right thing and keep that bag ready, we are in for a big catch," Steve shouting words of encouragement.

We then got all our equipment ready, descended into the darkness, and Steve positioned me, Doug, and Bruce about ten yards apart online. Steve had some last parting words of wisdom.

"Now you got to be patient. And make some noise and shake that light around in the bag so dem snipes will come your way," Steve insured us.

"I'm hungry," mumbled Doug.

"We just ate, Doug. Now focus, and you boys keep your eyes on the prize," said Steve.

"What does a snipe look like? I've never seen one," asked Bruce.

"It looks like a cross between a chicken and a blackbird, a red wing blackbird to be exact, cause like him, he is black and has little red wings, a rooster's head, and feet like a chicken," Steve described.

"Okay, fellas, we will holler at you when we need you to start making some noise. "You can go ahead and start practicing your snipe calls," Keith instructed the catching team.

"What does a snipe call sound like?" asked Bruce.

"Sort of a combination between a rooster crowing and a blackbird cawing. One after the other sort of all mixed up. I recommend one of you caw like a blackbird and the other two crow like a rooster, and that would be perfect," described Steve.

Keith and Steve started walking back toward Barton. A few minutes later, they gave us the signal, and like idiots, for the next thirty minutes, what seemed like forever, we made noise, cawing and crowing up a storm. As instructed, we were shaking our bags and flashlights and waiting on a bird that must not have made it onto Noah's ark. In other words, it didn't exist, at least not in these parts.

"I'm hungry. Let's go back and get something to eat," requested Doug.

"I got you Doug, Momma was making some peanut butter chewies and you can have some of those," I made his day with that revelation.

I dangled that carrot to entice Doug to hurry along but it really was not necessary as both him and Bru were baby brothers and pretty much conditioned to listen to their immediate chain of command which was their older brothers or older kids for direction.

"Cmon boys not sure what happened, but I don't think that there are any snipes in our fields. Let's go home, Let's call it a night." I said knowing we had been had once again by those two losers Steve and Keith" means.

On the long walk back, I started thinking about being a middle child and what that was like from my perspective.

I for one, being a middle child and having a younger and older brother experienced both sides of that equation which involved telling and being told.

In other words, I knew both sides of the gig. Age difference, gender, size and maturity level were pertinent factors as well. There was a four-year age difference between me and my older brother yet only a year and some change between me and little bro Bru. The same construct applied to Steve with him and his brothers Doug and Ricky.

Keith on the other hand was the top dog of his sibling chain and was accustomed to being in charge wherever and whenever. Speaking of middle children, what was the toughest thing for me was that I was always denied certain activities or things because my parents would answer my request in the negative one or two ways.

If I said Momma, " Can I get one of those balls like Bruce has then the answer would be "No son, you are too old for that" conversely if I asked Dad to go to see a movie with just friends and no parents or chaperones, like Brad was allowed to do, then the answer would be "No son, you are much too young for that sort of thing," Dad would say.

Okay A & J which is it? I would always think to myself after these canned denials but eventually I found a way to use them to my advantage.

Well enough on woe be me and middle child syndrome, bottom line was I had loving parents, a loving family and if I really wanted little bro

Bru's ball I could take it by force, just kidding, there were enough balls to go around so sharing was always a better option.

Back on Woodlawn we ran into Steve and Keith. Both were pretending nothing happened. T-bone had a new alias in my head. He was *Stoic Steve* his face just like Dallas Cowboy's Coach Tom Landry's face on the sidelines in a Dallas Cowboy nailbiter, said nothing. But that smirk on Keith's face said it all. As for us, as usual Doug's hunger pains took front and center and he or Bru for that matter did not seem to be bothered by what took place.

I was, and between the two of them. Keith and Steve, I was keeping score. On one side of the scorecard, I had written three entries: NASA comes to town, basketballs as key stones strategically placed in bridge supports and making me smell that sewage plant by telling me it was a pie factory. There would be four entries on my scorecard once I annotated Snipe hunting. No surprise to me that three of the four involved Keith as either a supporting function or lead. On the other side where I planned to get even it was a blank page, but I was not discouraged, I would get my chance to get even. Cousin Keith, your time is coming. A storm was coming, in fact a big storm, a tornado.

Momma always emphasized biding your time and I was doing just that.

Chapter 10

RESTAGING ACCIDENTS, THOSE PESKY PEARS, AND AN APPLE

It wasn't me!

One of the oldest tricks in the book is to try and fix or cover up your mistakes. We learned early on that all this did was make things worse and only buy time and prolong the inevitable consequence of being held accountable for our actions. Being avid wrestling fans, we were always tuned in on Saturday morning to listen to Banana Nose Lance Russell and Dave Brown as commentators and watch the wrestlers of the like of Jerry Lawler, Tojo Yamamoto, Jackie Fargo, and his crazy brother Nuthouse. I just loved that little old Black lady sitting on the front row with an umbrella that would beat those guys over the head. Just as we did after watching football games to run outside and play football, we did the same here. Yet we didn't have to go outside. We went at it right there in the den. The immediate vicinity would become our own personal wrasslin ring, complete with turnbuckles and all sorts of foreign objects. Instead of chairs, we used cushions as our foreign object to hit each other over the head. Pile drivers, sleeper holds, body slams, and attempts at figure fours were our main moves, but our favorite was the flying elbow drop with a leap from the couch to the living room floor on the exposed ribs of your opponent.

Of course, not everything went as planned, and during one of these impromptu bouts, we broke a lamp.

"Boy we are in for it now," I announced to the Fargo brothers Jackie and Roughhouse, Bru and Kurt, my cousin. Later Kurt and I would be known as the Blond Bombers.

"What are we gonna do?" asked Bru.

"I have a plan. We will prop it up as if it is good as new, and when Brad or Keith walk by and Momma is close by, I will nudge the table, and it will fall easily, break a second time, and we can then blame either one of them for breaking it,".

Again, what are brothers for?

Boys will be boys

As far as wrasslin, this roughhousing would continue all the way into early adulthood. It would be Big Phil demonstrating his strength when on a road trip for a softball tournament in Hope, Arkansas, a wrasslin bout broke out in a hotel room. The "boys will be boys," regardless of age, came to fruition when Butch Cook had David "Doc" Ross and Perry White in a headlock under each of his arms. Doc says suddenly, he looked down and saw Big Phil's head emerge between Butch's legs, and next thing he remembers, they were all airborne falling backward on the bed. Big Phil had lifted all three, Butch, Doc, and Perry, into the air. Falling backward on the bed, another piece of furniture became a victim to indoor wrasslin. The bed immediately broke into multiple pieces and was beyond repair. Time to load up the car and for the future Nasty Boys to make a getaway and head home. No restaging possible here.

Those pesky pears

- *Momma's pear tree bears fruit for the first time*

I told this story at my mom's graveside service in June summer of 2020. I finally had to come clean.

My mom once had a pear tree in the backyard, and she always told us not to play ball around that tree. The proud day comes when it finally starts to bear fruit, and the first pear appears on the tree. Of course, a few days later, what happens? We and a few of the guys are messing around, and *someone* threw a football into the tree, knocking off the most coveted pear on the planet. Time for a cover-up operation and to prolong the inevitable retribution from Momma.

"We did it again. How come every time you are around, we get into trouble, and I get the blame?" I shouted at Bruce.

"You are the one who knocked it off," Bruce shouted back.

"But you should have caught the ball," I countered. (Same old argument—if it's the QB or the receiver's fault for the incomplete pass, except this had more dire consequences.)

"It was you who broke the lamp and put a hook through my finger, so stop blaming me. I just happen to be around you every time you mess up, and that seems like a lot," Bru stated emphatically.

"Okay, here is what we are going to do. Run, get some tape while I grab a stool. The rest of you guys keep playing along as if nothing happened." Once again me devising the quick fix.

"Tape?" asked Bru.

"Just do it, time is short. She may come out here any minute and like dummies we are talking about it right next to the scene of the crime, the pear tree, go get the tape," I said adding "And don't ask her where the tape is, sneak it out and get clear tape at that."

So, Bruce ran and got some tape, and I grabbed a stool, and when he returned, I got on that stool, and I taped that pear back into its original position. Of course, a few days later, the not-ready-for-prime-time pear overripened and turned brown. Upon discovery by Momma, it was back to the interrogation room.

"Take a seat, son. Didn't I tell you not to play ball in the vicinity of that pear tree? Now you done gone and hurt the tree," began Momma.

"Yes, Momma, you sho did," I was trying to convince her I had heard her loud and clear.

"I'm not even going to ask what happened or who did it, but it is obvious someone disobeyed me and knocked that pear out of the tree playing ball or something," stated Momma.

I didn't want to lie to Momma, but isn't omission of certain and selective truths sort of like lying? I would take my punishment, but I also wanted Bruce to get some blame as well.

"Momma, me and some of the guys were throwing some footballs around, and the next thing I know, Bruce is standing over by the tree and beside him on the ground is the pear. I knew how much that pear meant to you, Momma, we all did. *Someone* thought it would be a good idea to buy us some time if we taped the pear back into the tree, and who knows, maybe we could save the pear. I think it was Bruce who got the tape and then *someone* taped the pear back into the tree. I'm sorry it didn't work. Man, that *someone* must be stupid," *Someone*, I murmured.

"Okay, I have heard enough, you know what comes next," said Momma ending the interrogation and moving on to the punishment phase.

"What about Bruce? Ain't he gittin' a lickin' as well?" I cried. (After all, misery loves company.)

"You worry about you. And to keep all this relative, I want you to go to that pear tree, find a branch, and bring it back, and it better be the right size," Momma instructed me.

To keep this relative, what is she talking about but now was not the time for me to start questioning Momma. Is there any more effective punishment and psychological warfare than having the guilty party be involved in and actively participating in the selection of the tool for torture and punishment that will be used against him? How to find that sweet spot and pick the right branch. On one hand, you don't want it to be too small because then the grim reaper, Momma, will go fetch a limb. And of course, you do not want it too big cause then it will hurt more. So, you hope for the best and go fetch a branch and return for the lashing.

And I thought to myself, *how ridiculous to say I hurt the tree*. That tree was not hurting. It was still standing and looked alive in my book, but I knew it was pointless to argue my case. My mind went back to the report card interrogation, and I knew it was useless to argue; just take my punishment. I deserved it this time.

So, I hoped for the best and went and got two switches. When I returned, Momma gave me the look.

"Why two? I said get one, "she said.

"I figured you might need an extra for Bruce," I cried.

She used both on me.

And that was that.

Many years later, about fifty, to be close to exact, I came clean during Mom's eulogy.

Telling the same story as above, I confessed.

June 5, 2020, at Mom's graveside.

"Momma, about that pear, that *someone* I kept referring to in the story, that *someone* was me,"

I could almost hear her say, "I know, son. Most questions I asked you, I already know the answers to."

• *Another pear story a few years later*

We had been messing around one summer night, up to no good, and someone called the po-po. Momma's pear tree had grown and given us many pears, and when the police showed up, me, Keith, and Bru were leaning up against the car. Keith was eating a pear. The policeman approached us and asked if we had seen anything suspicious.

"Have you boys witnessed anybody messing around the neighborhood, seems someone playing ding-dong ditch (ding-dong ditch is when you knock on someone's door and then run away before they answer it), and somebody called us. Someone even pooped in a bag, set it on a neighbor's porch, lit it on fire, and rang the doorbell. Now I got an angry neighbor who answered the door, stomped on a burning bag, and has crap all over his shoes. You fellas know anything about that?" the policeman asked.

"No, sir, I would never poop in a bag. I once pooped in the toilet display at Sears when I was little, but Momma wasn't mad. She was proud I was learning to do the number two somewhere other than my pants. Daddy said that was a tough one to live down, and his friends at work had a field day giving him the business the next couple of days. Said I should become a permanent part of the display, maybe they could sell more toilets. Wasn't my fault, what dummy puts up bathrooms in a store knowing little kids might need to go?" I rambled.

"Mr. Policeman, who got the poo on their shoe? Was it Old Man Donaldson or that other man with no hair that always tries to stiff us when we go to collect for our paper route? Maybe someone did it to Nasty Jim's house, he's a meanie too. We can call them poo on a shoe, sort of like cat on a hat," said Bru.

I gave Bruce a pinch on the leg to let him know to shut up.

Even dumber than I thought he was. Dumb as a box of rocks. We were not completely innocent in what was going down, like Sergeant Joe Friday used to say on Daddy's favorite TV show, we was complices. We had been having meetings with the gang, and it was decided to take Old Man D out. We was on a counterattack.

"You boys sound like you may have some enemies in this neighborhood. Are you sure you don't know anything about what's going on?" asked Mr. Policeman.

"Mr. Policeman, can I see your flashlight?" asked Keith.

"What for, son?" asked Mr. Policeman.

"I want to see if there is a worm in my pear," replied Keith. The policeman just smiled and left. "Kids these days," he muttered to himself. Besides, there were more important things to tend to.

- *The pear's cousin, Momo's apple tree*

Keith always climbing something, trying to get to a bird's nest.

Grandmother had a similar situation, except for her it was an apple tree. She was so excited, because like my momma was about her first pear, this was her first apple. Keith, my cousin, about six at the time, was visiting her and had received fair warning to not mess with that apple.

"Grandmother, look, your apple tree finally has an apple!" Keith shouted.

"It does, son, and I see you eyeing that apple. You are not allowed to pick that apple from the tree, do you understand?"

"Yes, ma'am," said Keith.

A few hours later, Momo looked up and saw that the apple was missing from her apple tree. She walked over and found the hard apple on the ground with a tiny set of teeth marks on one side. She immediately knew what had happened and called for Keith.

"Keith, get your little fanny out here," hollered Momo.

Keith, knowing that the game was up, came out with big crocodile tears running down his eyes.

"Didn't I tell you not to pick that apple?" asked Momo.

"Grandmother, I didn't pick that apple, I promise," said Keith.

"Son don't lie. You see the apple in my hand now, and I am sure these are your teeth marks," said Momo.

Crying uncontrollably, Keith said, "Grandmother, I promise I didn't pick that apple."

"Then you tell me how it got on the ground, and it is easy to see you tried to take a bite. Those are your teeth marks, aren't they?" said Momo

"Grandmother, I was never gonna pick the apple, and I didn't pick the apple. What happened was I just climbed up the tree and tried to take a small bite out of the apple, and it accidently fell out of the tree. Please don't spank me," cried a begging Keith.

Grandmother laughing to herself.

"It's okay, son, I should have explained myself better," admitted Momo.

• *Momma's dessert*

And finally, a positive pear story, one for the palate. Our favorite dessert was pear salad. Momma would take one of those juicy pears you got in a can, already halved, and place one on a leaf of iceberg lettuce on a small saucer. She would then add grated cheddar cheese, a touch of Miracle Whip, and a half cherry on the top. Not sure where Momma came up with this combination, but it worked. We loved it.

Chapter 11

OPERATION "NOW AND LATER"

The gang learned the hard way that one family moving away did not mean they would be replaced by the same type of people. Different people moving onto the street looked at their property differently and came with new rules and expectations. But one new neighbor who had recently moved in drew the ire of several of the boys. His name was Tommy Donaldson, Old Man D as the boys called him, and he would, when all was said and done, teach the boys some valuable lessons. As much as they tried to implement the Golden Rule and be good Christians, as Momma would preach, this man brought out the worst in the boys. Who did he think he was to come in on their beloved street and change the rules around? Yards were made to be played in, not put off-limits.

One day Momma was a bit shocked when out of the blue, Bruce started asking her questions. I was worried because again I felt he might compromise a secret operation we had in the works for Old Man D that we had planned the previous day.

"Momma how can a person be a bad egg?" asked Bru.

"Excuse me, son, what did you say?" Momma asked in return.

"Big Phil said Old Man D, er, I mean Mr. Donaldson is a bad egg. And Steve called Mr. Donaldson a mean cuss. I'm confused, is he a bad egg or cuss? And what's a cuss? I hear Big D say that sumtimes as well. Must mean sumptin'," said Bru.

"Why can't you boys let that man be? Bruce, what you are asking about are not so nice words, and you should not be using that kind of language. What are you boys up to? Bobby, what do you know about this?" questioned Momma.

Me praying that this was not the start of another of Momma's interrogations. "Oh, Momma, we just funnin' around. We mean no harm, and besides, even Daddy isn't crazy about our new neighbors. They ain't nothing like the Lynches. I wish they never moved," I whispered softly and sighed while squeezing my eyes shut with the beginning of a fake tear for added effect.

"That man has done nothing to you, boys, what's the problem?" continued Momma.

"Well, for one, I don't like the way he looks, he never smiles. And when we walk past his house, you better not even touch one blade of grass. Why does he love that yard so much anyway? He took away our end zone for our front yard games. He is as mean as that old man Boo Radley's father, Nathan Radley, in that book *To Kill a Mockingbird*. What's next, concrete in trees? Why can't he be like Mr. Rick?" I asked Momma.

"Son, he is a good man in his own kind of way. Not everyone can be like Mr. Rick. You must respect Mr. Donaldson and his property. And didn't I teach you better, not to judge people by how they look?" Momma reminded me.

"I will respect him, but I don't have to like him, and you still haven't told Bru what those words mean. I know what they mean, and I agree with the gang. He is a mean old man. I can't understand how someone could love a yard so much, look at our yard. We have no grass in the back from constant basketball games and playing. And besides, how he looks ain't the problem, it's his behavior,".

"Son, look at your behavior. You cannot always control how other people behave, but you can control your own behavior. As for yards, people have different ways of caring for their yard. Some people really love their yards. We found out long ago it's hard to have a nice yard and happy kids at the same time. Lucky for you, we went for happy kids,".

"Well, he has given us fair warnin' to stay off his yard, that he won the Yard of Merit, whatever that is, and we need to steer clear of his property," I said trying to get Momma on our side.

"Okay, son, just try and stay out of trouble," said Momma.

Little did Momma or Old Man D know we had our own operation that was in planning. We were planning a sniper operation. Old Man D's Yard of Merit sign was proudly put on display for all to see. The love and attention that sign got was even more than his yard. Every evening, he would wash it down and put it in a new location, most likely so people would take notice. Well, good for you, Old Man D, you and your highfalutin self. We now had a target. The sign. Yard of Merit. It better be cemented in and have round-the-clock protection because it was number one on our target list.

The Woodlawn Giant's planning session under the Spicer willow tree

Big Phil was sitting in his favorite chair with his huge glass of ice water and a plain box that was long and skinny.

"What's in the box, Big Phil?" asked Bru.

"Nothing special, I'll show you later. Fellas, I have had enuff of Old Man D. I don't even live close to him, and he gets on my nerves. We need to put him in his place," Big Phil announced.

"I have an idea, he just loves dat sign. We got to do something about dat sign, any ideas?" Steve asked the gang.

"We could always just take it and stick it in Nasty Jim's yard," answered Ricky.

"That's a good idea, but let's hold that thought for later. That can come in a later phase of the operation," Steve queried the gang.

"What are fazes?" asked Bru.

"Phases are when we do different things at different times. Back to planning," Steve described.

"I like that, Steve; I have an idea, but what are the rest of you thinking?" pondered Big Phil.

"We need to do something, so he feels immediate pain. Somehow, we get at his sign and deface it while he is right there and must witness it. I would luv to see his face when we mess up his precious sign. He treats that thing like it belongs in a museum," Mark chimed in.

"That is a great idea, but how can we pull that off?" Steve wondered out loud.

"Well, Mark is good at findin' his mark with bricks. He did hit my head that time when me and Ricky were building forts for our G.I. Joe. He is also a punt, pass, and kick champeen. Surely, if he can throw a football dat far and accurate, he can hit dat sign with rocks. Perhaps we can throw rocks at the sign from behind the bushes while Old Man D is working in his so beautiful yard (said very sarcastically). Dat way we mark up his sign and get rocks in his yard as well. Dat will surely teach him," I shouted.

"Bobby, the only reason Mark's brick found its mark was because it was drawn to dat shiny light of a hed you have. Dat tow hed of yours is shiner than the diamonds in Hope," laughed Steve.

"Although I would love to hammer that sign with rocks, it's too risky. Let's go to the brains of this group. Brad, what do you think?" asked Mark.

"Well, I think what we need, fellas, is a sniper operation, someone as a spotter and someone with a gun so we can hit the sign from far away and remain undetected," declared Brad.

"That's what I was waiting to hear. Check this out, fellas," Big Phil said grinning as he picked up the box.

He then reached into the box and pulled out his new pellet gun.

"I can pockmark that sign from a distance, and Old Man D will never know from where it is coming. Who wants to be my spotter?" threw out Big Phil and the hands immediately flew up in response.

"I'm hungry," said Doug.

"Well, it can't be you, Doug. You can't make it that long without food. Hattie must live in the kitchen to keep you fed," Big Phil laughed.

"I can't hep I'm always hungry," muttered Doug.

"Be quiet, Doug. Since we are gonna be planning this operation for a while, and it is hot as Hades out here, why don't you and Bru grab that wagon full of empty Coke bottles and haul them up to Ingram and trade them in for money and bring the gang back some goodies. Back to phases, phases are just different things we do at different times starting with the beginning of our operation and then the end game. Phase one is you two on a supply run. I declare you the logistics team. Fellas, put in your order. These two gonna run up to Nite and Day and bring us back some goodies. And, Doug, no pit stops at Coleman's for a pork barbecue sandwich," Steve directed to the two youngest gang members.

"I want some M&M's," said Mark.

"Red Hots for me," added Brad.

"Sugar Babies and Sweet Tarts, that's my sweet and sour," said Rod.

"Hershey's bar," said Big Phil.

"Get Lemonheads for Cobb (Bobby). They match that nugget of his and Tootze (Ricky) a Tootsie Roll," never one for a simple yes or no added Steve.

"Thanks, T-bone, maybe you can get Milk Duds since you are a dud, or how about Whoppers for all those lies you tell," I countered.

"Or maybe a candy necklace for one of those Smith girls down the street. Which one do you like, Bobby? I think Steve likes Sylvia. S and S has a nice ring. Steve and Sylvia sittin in a tree, K-I-S-S-I-N-G," laughed Ricky.

And the whole crowd joined in:

All the boys except Steve chorused, "First comes love, then comes marriage, here comes Steve with a baby carriage."

"I like Janice, I call her Skillet cause she's tough," I admitted.

Right after I said it, I knew I had messed up and let the cat out of the bag. Following suit to Steve, I had also outed myself for that horrible sin of liking a girl.

It was my turn to be on the wrong side of the K-I-S-S-I-N-G diddy

All the boys were ribbing Steve and me now. Associating with girls was a no-no. Like Spanky and Our Gang, they were avid members and sworn to the He-Man Woman-Haters Club.

Big Phil settled the gang back down. "Okay, enuff ribbin, fellas, back to planning."

"As for our operation, let's give it a proper name. How about *Now and Later* since we are planning *now* and gonna execute *later*," Ricky propositioned.

"Awesome, Ricky, we will name our operation *Now and Later*," Big Phil concluded.

"Okay, Doug and Bru, just grab all the candy you can and take that cooler over there and bring back soda water. Make sure it's Coke. No Pepsis, and add some Dr. Peppers, and be sure and ice em down," ordered Steve.

"I could be a good spotter. I got some binos as well and some walkie-talkies, so we can talk," I said, looking through imaginary binos and then talking through a make-believe walkie-talkie for added effect.

"Can't be you, Bobby. With that tow head and crew cut, the sun and moon always reflect off your head and gives your position away. Remember last night playing hide-and-seek, I saw your reflection a mile away," joked Steve.

At this point Brad intervened. "It was my idea, and me and Big Phil are the oldest, so we will be the sniper team. Phil the shooter, and me the spotter. Now no one says anything. This Saturday morning, we know where Old Man D will be, out in that yard mowing away, and we will launch fires on his beloved sign. If Phil can toss a forty-five all the way to the Stevenses' house, I am sure with a rifle, he can reach Old Man D's sign with a pellet. Bobby, you and Ricky can be on the reconnaissance team. Watch Old Man D from our back porch and relay to me and Big Phil when he is almost finished in the back and moving towards to the front so we can get ready," Brad instructed laying out the details.

Wrapping up the meeting, there was no Atticus Finch that day to lecture us on what to do and what not to do with guns and to never kill a mockingbird, set some parameters. We would not have cared anyway. We had a mission, a real operation, *Now and Later*. Saturday morning came, and like clockwork, that meanie OMD would shortly be out there mowing his grass.

Many of those not privileged enough to be actively involved in the operation did not want to miss out on the fun. They wanted to watch the events unfold from what undoubtedly was our biggest shenanigan to date and had found various ways to observe the operation from different vantage points. Some had climbed trees, some were on roofs, and some luckier ones had a line of sight on the target from their bedroom windows. This was huge. This was a step up from ding-dong ditch or rolling someone's yard with toilet paper.

Me and Ricky were on the back porch, staking out Old Man D, and Brad and Big Phil were on the carport of Big Phil's house, waiting for the transmission. We had developed key code words for our operation. I had covered my head with a beanie to prevent any light reflecting off my head and had my favorite army camouflage poncho that we were under.

Reconnaissance team members Tootsie and Cobb, Ricky and Bobby:

Ricky said in his walkie-talkie to sniper team Big Phil and Brad, "Ralphie and Big Guy, we have sighted the goat eating grass in the rear." (Translation: Brad and Big Phil, we see Old Man D mowing grass in his backyard.)

"OMD is almost done. Relay the next message to the sniper team," I whispered to Ricky.

"The goat is almost done eating grass in the rear," Ricky said to snipers. (Translation: Old Man D is almost finished mowing in the back and will soon be moving to the front yard.)

Team sniper was now in position. Big Phil had loaded up his pellet gun, with Brad by his side as a spotter.

"Goat has wandered off to a new pasture," Ricky said to sniper team. (Translation: Old Man D is now moving to his front yard.)

"Well, there he is like clockwork, getting ready to mow what he considers his masterpiece. He is so predictable. Soon he will be moving over to pull up his beloved Yard of Merit sign so he can even get to the grass around the pole supporting it. Then he will reposition it in another part of the yard invariably so people who have seen it once will look all over for it just to see it a second time. What a vain grass-loving clown," Big Phil stated in unison of taking aim with his pellet gun.

"Yeah, he is moving towards the sign, time to let her rip. Fire the first shot," Brad said tapping him on his left shoulder which was the sign to shoot.

Old Man Donaldson was walking toward his yard of merit sign and suddenly heard a ping.

"Perfect shot, now fire for effect. Seems OMD is startled," Brad excitedly uttered to Phil again tapping him on his left shoulder.

At that time on, what would have made the Rifleman proud, Big Phil started firing repeatedly and unloading on the sign.

Ping, ping, ping, the pellets sang as they started finding their mark and peppering OMD's Rembrandt.

"What in the world is going on here, I am under attack," cried a startled OMD.

Fearing for his safety, he then ran in a zigzag motion, like he was personally under fire himself in a combat zone, back into the house.

It had to be one of the funniest things we had ever seen, and let's just say the gang got a good laugh. Seeing OMD running around in his front yard was a sight to see. Apparently, OMD called the cops, because they showed up, but we all were sworn to silence on this one.

The West Memphis Police Department didn't think it was worth their time or money to conduct a full-blown investigation on this incident, or perhaps there was no pellet gun ballistics department of experts to determine a guilty party, because we heard nothing from them.

OMD petitioned the city for a new sign. It was replaced, but we were done. At least most of us.

Later at our next meeting and an after-action review of sorts to go over how operation Now and Later had gone, we decided that was enough. We had made our point and so far, gotten away with it, so why push our luck.

"Fellas, we were successful and escaped justice, so I say on to bigger and better things," said Big Phil.

Everyone agreed except Steve, who was the one who always had an extra card up the sleeve.

"Look, one final action, and we can call it quits," said Steve.

"What now, T-bone? You always seem to come up wit great ideas, but us other guys must do your dirty work, and we end up getting in trouble while, of course, you escape scot-free," I pointed out.

"Hear me out, Cobb. This is low risk, and all you gotta do is run into his yard at night under the cover of darkness when no one can see you, pull up his sign, and run across the street and stick it in Nasty Jim's yard. I will be on lookout," said Steve. (If there were ever two yards more different than OMD's yard and Nasty Jim's yard, then one would be hard-pressed to find them. Simply put, one was immaculate and, give credit where credit is due, the city's Yard of Merit. The other looked like something akin to Fred Sanford's yard—full of junk, complete with junkyard dogs and all other kind of stuff.)

"If it's dark and no one can see me, why do I need a lookout? Why don't you grab the sign, and I will be on the lookout? Besides, me and Ricky proved in the last operation what great reconnaissance men we are. Count me out on this one. I have been in enuff trouble lately. Momma sez that game Trouble, those folks owe us money 'cause dat game is named after me," I opted out,

So that was that. None of the fellas wanted to push their luck, and if this was to happen, it would have to be a solo operation.

And apparently, it was because one morning, I woke up, and as I was walking to school, what did I see? One of the nastiest yards in the city with a coveted Yard of Merit sign.

Congratulations, Nasty Jim.

As far as I can remember, that was the last incident with the Yard of Merit sign. Like most boys, we had a short attention span and moved on to other things.

Chapter 12

TELEVISION, SIMPLE PASTIMES

Television

One TV and one set of rabbit ears, with only three major network channels, ABC, CBS, and NBC and a local public broadcasting station, PBS channel on 10, did not equate to a lot of television watching on Woodlawn. Besides, we spent most of our time outside. When reception would screw up, which honestly didn't seem that often, even the stations experiencing technical difficulties were polite and let you know to please stand by, which would flash across the screen. (I would tell Bruce that meant he had to literally stand by the television for it to work again). When you got that message, at least you knew it wasn't you, and there was no need for troubleshooting such as repositioning the rabbit ears or adding aluminum foil.

The commercials were so much better as well. We didn't have to wait for Super Bowl Sunday for special commercials; they were on all the time. Some of my favorites:

Charmin toilet paper

Mr. Whipple setting those rules he could not live by him-self, telling the customers to not squeeze the Charmin, snatching it away from the customer and then inadvertently squeezing it himself.

Reese's Peanut Butter Cup

Or how about the two guys, one who loved chocolate and the other who loved peanut butter walking around a corner and bumping into each other.

"Hey, you got chocolate on my peanut butter," said guy 1. "Hey, you got peanut butter on my chocolate," said guy 2. Guy 1 and 2 said, "Wow, this tastes good."

What were some of your favorites? Below is a little quiz I made to take you down memory lane of some of my other favorites, which I am sure you liked as well. I also added some of my favorite shows, movies, and other memorable television moments. Match the lettered items on the left with the proper phrases or things on the right:

A. Life cereal____ Tan, don't burn use Copper Tone, lil girl and her dog
B. Rolaids____ Cartoon of cat and mouse
C. Peacock changing colors____ MGM opening for a movie
D. Wide World of Sports____ Miller Lite, "Taste Great, Less Filling," showing off
E. Coca-Cola commercial____ "Give it to Mikey, he likes it"!
F. Jody Foster____ "I wish cotton was a monkey," a Little Rascal
G. Cigarette ad with cowboy____ NBC
H. Steve Mizerak "the Miz"____ "Plop, plop, fizz, fizz, oh what a relief it is."
I. Stymie____ "I'd like to teach the world to sing in perfect harmony"
J. Tom and Jerry____ Marlboro Man
K. Lion roaring____ Thrill of victory and agony of defeat, Jim McKay

Other forms of entertainment—paper and cardboard

If not playing sports or watching TV, we found other ways to keep ourselves occupied outdoors, and, if raining, indoors. A lazy afternoon would be one spent laying in the yard and looking for four-leaf clovers. How many kids do you know that are aware that there are four-leaf clovers, much less have found them? Paper and cardboard were inexpensive material for constructing toys. Whenever someone on the street would purchase a large appliance, then the box it was delivered in instantly became a prized possession. A box in original form could be used for building forts. After that, it could be cut up and dismantled to be used to construct makeshift sleds. We didn't have much snow in our part of Arkansas. Additionally, living in a flood plain, we had no hills. But we did have overpasses and the levee, and sliding down those on cardboard was the next best thing. Except for Doug with whom even playing with something as harmless as cardboard backfired. He had slid down the incline of the bayou, gone over some glass, and ended up with a cut to the butt. Doug as mentioned earlier was second only to me in childhood injuries.

Origami paper finger game

How many of you ever made an origami paper finger game, remember those? A paper fortune-teller. I remember it always seemed to be girls running around with these things with their hidden messages, ready to read your fortune. I must have always picked the wrong girl, or she intentionally loaded her fortune-teller with nothing but negative messages, because all I ever got was gloom and doom predictions. Perhaps that is why I was continuously involved in so many accidents.

Paper football

Or paper football, that tabletop game requiring only a sheet of paper folded into a small triangle slid back and forth across a table. A touchdown was when part of the football hung over the edge without falling off, or you could elect for a field goal and kick the football through your opponent's constructed goal posts which were his hands pointing downward to the table and thumbs extended and joined. I remember it was Brad and Ken Stafford that taught me and Bruce how to play. What a simple game, and what fun.

Our first electronic games

Electric football was another fun one. I can remember tapping behind the players to make them move faster. I remember one year we found one of these games hidden under Momma's bed, what was supposed to be a Christmas present. I bet we got twenty games in before Santa officially delivered that present.

Before the nerf

Long before we had our first nerf basketball hoop, we made our own indoor basketball hoop. A simple coffee can with both ends cut out was our goal, and a plastic ball as the pill was all we needed for epic hallway games.

Board games

Only one—Monopoly. For Monopoly, I always wanted to be the car. What was your favorite piece? What was your favorite property?

The message here is there is always something to do. We seemed to find ways to pass our time.

Chapter 13

ALL THINGS MUST PASS AND THE CIRCLE OF LIFE

Growing up, moving away, goodbye, and hello again

I cried when the Spicer family moved away.

There comes that day when we all start moving on. We grow up, we move away. We lose touch. As you grow, your world grows with you. You go to new places, and you make new friends. Your reach is expanded, and you experience new things and meet new people. It was no different for us as we got older, and our little world, initially defined and limited to the street where we lived, started branching out. Institutions like schools and church expose one to new teachings, but more importantly, new people. As you move through the educational system of kindergarten, elementary, junior and then senior high, that group of new people progressively gets larger and larger. We soon learned that there was a larger world out there beyond the confines of our street and our group of friends. We were Woodlawn Giants, but there were other groups of people out there as well.

But things were changing within the confines of our own street as well. For us Giants on Woodlawn, our first major wake-up call to inevitable change to our innocent world was the Spicer family of Mark, Ricky, Mrs. Mary Jane, and Mr. Rick moving away to Westwood Acres, all the way on the other side of town. It might as well have been across the country. It really seemed that far.

I remember, like I always did when looking for answers, to go ask Momma.

"Momma, I don't understand. The whole family is runnin' away, why? With no Mr. Rick, who's gonna be our new groundskeeper?" I cried.

"Son, these are one of those things you will learn for yourself as you grow up. I am sure it is a hard decision for their family, but it is what they think is best for their family,".

"But what about our family, how can they leave us like that? I bet Mark and Rick don't wanna go. Parents always making their kids do stuff they don't wanna do, it ain't fair!" I exclaimed.

"Again, son, one day it will be clearer to you, and you will understand, and besides, a new family will move in, and you will make new friends,".

This was not Momma just trying to let me down easy. I was not the only one who was upset. Our two families were more than just friendly neighbors. Dad and Mr. Rick were fishing buddies, fellow groundskeepers for our various sports complexes, Momma and Mrs. Mary Jane were the best of friends, our families vacationed together and even more the pines planted extended the entire length of both the Williams' and Spicer's backyard rear property lines as a symbol of connecting the two families.

I was not finished and continued.

"Yeah, well perhaps, but I bet their daddy won't be like Mr. Rick, and I know their momma will not be like Mrs. Mary Jane. And no one can replace Mark and Ricky," I countered.

As for the new neighbors moving in, I don't recall who they were or if they even had kids. That spoke volumes and tells you something. I'm not saying that is good or bad, just different. It was the beginning of an end to an era.

And in the queue? Us. Our family, the Williams, would follow suit a few years later, and I can tell you it was not an easy sell to convince us to leave our paradise. I was in total shock when I found out we were moving. Now I really needed some explanation, and Momma better have some good answers. Like Lucy, she had some *splaining* to do. Going in to confront Momma, I felt my argument was rock-solid. The Ten-Mile Bayou was my long pole in the tent and the crux of my reasoning to stay put and not to move.

"Is it true, are we now the ones moving?" I shouted.

"Yes, son, we are and you can lower your voice," answered Momma.

"I sort of understand how you explained why the Spicers moved, but that was for them. Why are we moving? Look at this place. What about the bayou? How can we leave that behind? It's so close here," I pointed out.

"Son, don't you worry, there are more bayous out there in this big world for you to explore," said Momma.

"Momma, what about those pine trees Mr. Rick and Daddy planted? Who is gonna take care of those?" I asked her.

Just like Momma said the pines still stand and are just fine in 2021.

"Son, don't you worry. Just like bayous, there are more trees for you to get attached to, and those pines will be fine. And you will have a shorter walk to school, East will be right across the field. And you will be closer to Buck," replied Momma.

"Buck is Bruce's friend, and anyway, I ain't moving. Steve said I could move in with them."

"That's okay, son, go ahead and pack your stuff and move on down there. I'll help you, but you need to go now. I am getting ready to fry some chicken and finish up with my soup beans and then make cornbread. And of course, my freshly brewed tea needs to be replenished to wash all that down," said Momma.

"I think I'll stay for now," I decided.

Momma won that battle, and our family then moved westward closer toward East Junior High, setting up stakes on Wilson Road. We boys survived, and we made new friends like the Harts, Kyle and Frankie, Michael and Teresa Price, Tony and Vickie Lacefield, Dennis and Hope Ellis, David Pickett, and Ricky Brickey. There would also be some new Mr. Rick Spicer replacements, some new father figures to enter the equation as well. Men like Mr. Dewey Hart and Mr. Jimmy Lee Price. I became close friends with Frankie and Kyle and remember my trips to Kaycee, Mississippi, hunting dove and hanging out with Frankie at Dewey Senior's house. And it was Jimmy Lee, Michael's father, who was a second father to all of us boys. Working at Universal Warehouse was a rite of passage for all of us, and putting up with the likes of us to include them Mississippi boys like Jimmy Don and Rory kept Jimmy Lee's head on a swivel. I loved that man, and every time I was home on leave, I would make a special trip to go see him. Both Jimmy Lee and Dewey Senior were special men. Jimmy Lee has passed, but Mr. Hart, in his nineties, is still with us as I write this. God bless both.

I know one person particularly happy about the move, and that was Jimmy Buchanan, known as Buck. It meant that he would be closer to Bruce (we call them the life partners, eep). Seriously, Buck was like another son and brother in our family. My parents loved him like he was one of their own. As for my parents, everyone loved them. Adolph and Joyce were referred to as A and J. Everyone loved Momma's tea, which Randy referred to as cow soup. If other kids like your parents, that should tell you something, like you are blessed and how lucky you are. We were. Buck was there as a pallbearer for Momma when she passed away in the summer of '20. We love you, Buck; you will always be a brother.

As we got even older, our worlds expanded even more, and it was kids from our world from the east side meeting those from the western and southern parts of town, courtesy of senior high. I met people like David "Doc" Ross, Jeff Spencer, Rusty Langley, Doug Poe, Terry Davis, John "Bubba Hut" Vernon, Kathy Brazil—the list goes on. My east side friends were Barbara Robinson, Susan Ball, Janice Smith, Pam Gately Gray, and her brother, my best friend at Maddux, Jimmy, Marty "Oral Hershiser" Stevens, "We don't want you around" David Picket and Rich Busby. The list is endless, and all are great Americans. And as you move on after high school, the list grows even more. You go on journeys, starting with the senior trip. What a memory as me, Terry Davis, Bubba Mills, Kathy Brazil, and Rochelle Butler went to Panama City Beach. Ask Terry about that trip.

I always looked for ways to get to West Memphis, but sometimes West Memphis found me.

As I got older and moved away, I always found ways to get back home to West Memphis. Sometimes I would go to extremes, like taking off from Fort Chaffee, Arkansas, and driving to West Memphis with my army buddy, Roger Shuck. We had no civilian clothes, so Uncle Larry Joe took us to Kmart and hooked us up. It may have been almost like wearing Garanimals, but it worked. We had a great time, and Roger got to meet my family, especially Uncle Larry and his friends Travis and RL.

Other times, I could be in the most faraway places and run into fellow West Memphians. Like California where I lived with Tim Maness, sort of an Oscar and Felix arrangement, in Salinas and later in Ventura, California, with Tony Lacefield. He had told me he was coming, but I didn't believe him until he showed up on my doorstep. What do you do? Well, you open the door and say "come on in." Another time, my brother Bruce, Randy Arms, and Daryl Livingston came for a stay in Ventura, California. What a road trip across I-40 that must have been.

One great example of West Memphis finding me was Doug Poe. At the time, I was stationed in Estonia. How cool is that to be stationed in a faraway place like Estonia, and a friend you graduated high school with comes to Europe and makes you part of his itinerary. We had a great visit, and it was so nice for me to spend that time with him, and of course, we reminisced about our time as Blue Devils.

But the most surprising of all was me linking up with no other than my number one nemesis from Woodlawn. The lovely, high-spirited, larger-than-life Janice Smith, Skillet. Yes, the same Skillet that used to always give me the business back in the day in the hood. Of all places, thirty plus years after meeting in West Memphis, we were reunited in Tallahassee, Florida. It was great hooking up with her and thinking back to our days as kids on Woodlawn.

I have enjoyed this opportunity to reflect on my time on Woodlawn and West Memphis, Arkansas, and feel very fortunate to grow up with all these special and wonderful people. Whenever I go home, I always ride over to the street just to see the houses. I then ride down Barton toward Stuart and glance back toward the pines. They are so tall now, still standing after all these years just like Momma said they would be.

And when I look at them, I think of those little boys that grew into men. Each tree I have assigned to one of you Giants. Big Phil, you, Perry White, Doug Sutton, Doug White, and Bill Drennan may be gone now, but your spirit lives on in those trees and in our hearts. Love you, Big Phil. Rest in peace, but not too much; you need to keep those boys in line up there.

As for the rest of you still with us, Mark and Ricky, Steve, Rodney, and my brothers Bruce and Brad, and my cousin Keith, this book is for you. I hope, like it did for me, it brings back special memories. I would love before we all make our next big move that we get together sometime and reminisce on that wonderful period in our life. I am sure Big Phil is looking down on us all and holding down the fort. Someday, all the Woodlawn Giants will be reunited.

THE END

Me on finishing this book and reflecting on those who have passed.

ABOUT THE AUTHOR

Robert Ross Williams is a retired army officer living in Annandale, Virginia. Mr. Williams has a B.A. in Anthropology from the University of Memphis and a M.A. in Russian studies from Florida State University.

www.ingramcontent.com/pod-product-compliance
Lightning Source LLC
LaVergne TN
LVHW061529070526
838199LV00009B/432